MW01505720

PRAISE FOR
BEYOND OUTRAGE

"In an age marked by spin, exaggeration, and outright fabrication, Michael Philliber equips Christians to engage media with both discernment and charity. A master class in wisdom."
-Dustin Messer, Vicar of All Saints Dallas

"In *Beyond Outrage* Mike Philliber provides a needed correction for an age where an inaccurate report from a favored media outlet can fuel inappropriate - and contagious - outrage. Applying the eight common sense (but not commonly followed) practices he advocates to vet the information we see and read would lower the temperature of the rhetoric that characterizes our increasingly polarized society."
-Dr. Larry Hoop, *byFaith* News Editor

"Everyone recognizes that there is something wrong with our current media situation, both traditional media, such as television and newspapers, as well as social media. Anger and outrage rule the day. But no one seems to have any idea about how to change that. In this book, Philliber offers a clear solution to the problem: Validate before you palpitate, authenticate before you propagate. He clearly explains what that means and gives the reader practice in doing just that. Though written particularly for Christians, the book will help anyone concerned not just with the issue in general but with one's own response."

-Ben Shaw, Professor of Old Testament at Reformation Bible College.

"Rev. Philliber has provided us with a wise and winsome defense against the avalanche of 'news' that slams us daily. In the spirit of the prophet Isaiah's warning not to call conspiracy all that this people calls conspiracy, and not to fear what they fear, this book urges us to honor the Lord of hosts and to find hope in his sanctuary."

-Rev. Marq Toombs Associate Pastor, Redeemer Rockwall, Rockwall, Texas.

"In *Beyond Outrage* Mike Philliber has given us a massive application of the 9th commandment! Here his gobs of reading, research, and examples are gathered up, assessed, digested, and packaged in one concise manual that would make a superb elective study for your church group. He doesn't offer a prescription for all your troubles—only how to keep your head in deceptive and deranged times."

-Dale Ralph Davis, Author, Former Professor of Old Testament at Reformed Theological Seminary, Retired Minister.

"There is no doubt that we are in an age where the challenge of responding to the issues of the day with Biblical clarity and charity is, to say the least, overwhelming. The Biblical principal and practical insights coming from Michael Philliber's volume is beyond valuable. The content and the presentation are both informative and captivating. Thanking the Lord that He has allowed His wisdom to not only be displayed in Michael's ministry but now conveyed in this crucial volume. Get it – Read it – Use it!"

- Harry L Reeder, III, Sr. Pastor, Briarwood Presbyterian Church

BEYOND OUTRAGE

VETTING MEDIA TO INCREASE SENSIBILITY AND STABILITY

Michael W. Philliber

NEW HARBOR PRESS

RAPID CITY, SD

Copyright © 2023 Michael W. Philliber.

All rights reserved. No part of this publication may be reproduced, distributed or transmitted in any form or by any means, including photocopying, recording, or other electronic or mechanical methods, without the prior written permission of the publisher, except in the case of brief quotations embodied in critical reviews and certain other noncommercial uses permitted by copyright law. For permission requests, write to the publisher, addressed "Attention: Permissions Coordinator," at the address below.

Philliber/New Harbor Press
1601 Mt. Rushmore Rd, Ste 3288
Rapid City, SD 57701
NewHarborPress.com

Ordering Information:
Quantity sales. Special discounts are available on quantity purchases by corporations, associations, and others. For details, contact the "Special Sales Department" at the address above.

Beyond Outrage / Michael W. Philliber. -- 1st ed.
ISBN 978-1-63357-270-6

CONTENTS

Praise for Beyond Outrage i

Foreword 1

Introduction: Story, Scheme, Structure, and Scriptures 7

Anger, Anxiety, and Awe 23

Accusation Does Not Mean Guilt 41

Guilty until Proven Innocent? 51

Interlude: Humility 63

Suspend Judgment 69

Interlude: Posting with Peacemaking on the Brain 87

Hanlon's Razor 93

Human Reporters 107

Interlude: Grandstanding 121

Reasonable Explanations 129

Interlude: Writing Charitably 141

Media Angle 147

Overreporting 161

Final Interlude: The Violence Project 181

It's a Wrap! 187

Bibliography 197

Index 205

FOREWORD

"You are a human animal; you are a very special breed; for you are the only animal, who can think, who can reason, who can read"—so goes the Disney video. And long ago Aristotle noted the same: "it is the special property of man in distinction from the other animals that he alone has perception of good and bad and right and wrong and the other moral qualities, and it is partnership in these things that makes a household and a city-state" (Aristotle, *Politics*, 1253*a*).

But what does it mean to exercise those distinctively human capacities? Most of us know that it takes place in communities, through conversation. But are we properly equipped to play our part?

We can focus this with an appeal to the authority of St Eeyore in the Sacred Pooh canon, in the story "In which Eeyore finds the Wolery and Owl moves into it" (ch. 9 of The House at Pooh Corner):[1]

---

1. Dutton edition (1994), p. 314.

"Not *conversing*," said Eeyore. "Not *first one and then the other*. You said 'Hallo' and Flashed Past. I saw your tail a hundred yards up the hill as I was meditating my reply. I had thought of saying 'What?' — but, of course, it was then too late."

"Well, I was in a hurry." [said Rabbit]

"No *Give and Take*," Eeyore went on. "No *Exchange of Thought*. 'Hallo—What"— I mean, it gets you nowhere, particularly if the other person's tail is only just in sight for the second half of the conversation."

To converse as Eeyore describes it is to respect the human dignity of our neighbor. Such exchanges of thought can convey our affection, or enlist sympathy, or reassure, or simply inform. But they can also offer *argument*, the effort to persuade another person by a string of reasoning. To engage in such a back-and-forth is to risk having one's mind changed, in all humility. Even if the argument does not persuade, it can still promote mutual understanding. To do this both *requires* some kind of empathy ("what is it like to be you and to think the way you do?"), and *promotes* further empathy.

Sadly, much of what goes by the name of "argument" in our current setting is not the genuine exchange of thought, of give-and-take, of epistemic risk and humility; it is more often the assertion of the different sides' moral and intellectual superiority over each other; it is geared toward raising the morale of "our side" and placing the opposition firmly in the camp of the "repugnant cultural other."[2]

Remarking on Proverbs 27:17 ("Iron sharpens iron, and one man sharpens another"), Derek Kidner mentions what he calls "the healthy clash of personalities or views": "A true friendship," he explains, "should have both elements, the reassuring and the bracing."[3] In promoting our ability to think clearly, read clearly, write clearly, and speak clearly, we are really promoting the conditions for a healthy social system—a system in which strong friendships may flourish.

2. Alan Jacobs uses this term in *How to Think: A Survival Guide for a World at Odds* (New York: Currency, 2017), 26, who in turn derived it from sociological studies.
3. Derek Kidner, *Proverbs*, TOTC (Downers Grove: IVP, 1964), 45.

Dr Philliber wants to equip you with the tools for practicing this aspect of "virtue." He went public with his book, *Our Heads on Straight: Sober-Mindedness—A Forgotten Christian Virtue* (2021), where he shows that thinking clearly—which includes charity and calmness—is a vital part of the virtue the Lord wants to form within us, so that we, the community of his cherished people, can really flourish as God would have us do. It's a point that needs making, and he made it well!

Having made that broad point so effectively, he now offers us this very practical guide to one aspect of conversing, namely how we respond to reports about others: "validate before you palpitate, authenticate before you propagate." He says, "If you can grasp this perception, ...

You will be able to vet the media, assess news sources, and evaluate social media posts and tweets in such a way as to increase your stability. You will be able to move beyond outrage!

He certainly delivers on these promises; but I don't want you to miss how much more he's giving you. He's expounding a set of moral and relational disciplines that will affect the whole of your life; if you take his advice to heart, and encourage your community to do so as well, you will find that genuine health will follow, with people able to converse, to disagree, to listen, to grow together in serving the Savior.

Following Dr Philliber's principles will equip you to function faithfully in your local community, as well as in the wider bodies of which you are a part—both religious and civic. Indeed, I think you will be happier at home!

Dr Philliber has plenty of years of military and then pastoral experience under his belt, and his wisdom is clear. I know him mostly through online activities, where I can see that he walks the talk. His book on sober-mindedness came to me just as I was creating a seminary class on "Thinking, Reading, Writing, and Speaking Well," unfortunately too late for me to require it in the class. Next time I teach it, however, I intend to use that one as well as the one you are now holding.

I am sure that as you read you will feel a firm, wise, and gentle voice guiding you into a fuller exercise of your God-given humanity, and that you will like and admire Dr Philliber as I have come to do.

OK, enough from me; let me get out of the way and wish you good hunting (as they say in Kipling's *Jungle Books*), and every blessing!

—C. John Collins, Professor of Old Testament,
Covenant Theological Seminary
St. Louis, Missouri

INTRODUCTION: STORY, SCHEME, STRUCTURE, AND SCRIPTURES

The whole point of this little work is packaged in one simple concept: <u>Validate before you palpitate; authenticate before you propagate</u>. That's it. Short, sweet, and simple. If you can grasp this perception, you have the point of the whole book. You will be able to vet the media, assess news sources, and evaluate social media posts and tweets in such a way as to increase your sensibility and stability. You will be able to move beyond outrage! Before I define my simple concept, let me tell you a story about a distant relative.

The Story

I'm going to withhold names, but this person gave me permission to tell his story. I'm calling him Stan. I've done my research, reading the accounts and news sources that confirm his story.

Stan is a distant relative of mine, though he's in a different branch of the family. His clan and mine split in the late 1700s. Mine went south and ended up in Oklahoma, while Stan's stayed where it was. In July 2019, he was accused of stealing over $350,000 in cash and assets from an elderly woman that he cared for, a woman who treated him like family and whom he took care of. This care and friendship unfolded over many years. After she died, an estranged son of the woman came to town seemingly from nowhere and made the accusation. The police, the District Attorney, and the courts got involved. Stan ended up spending months in jail before any court trial, and the local paper publicized the allegations as big news. The case ground on for a year and a half. According to my relative, many people in the township read the allegations in the local tabloid and began to avoid him, turned a cold shoulder toward him, and finally cut him out of several of their social networks. It seemed that in their minds he was guilty because the accusations were printed in the paper.

After some time, and several court appearances, it became glaringly evident that Stan had not done any of the things he had been accused of, and he was cleared of all charges. His case never even went to a jury trial and the District Attorney was finally heard to say, "There's nothing here." After the case was dismissed, Stan's father went to the same local newspaper that had publicized the accusations as big news. When Stan's father requested that the same media source publish an article announcing that all the allegations against Stan had been dropped, his requests were rebuffed on the grounds that this was not news. I don't know about you, but I think that would be great news. I'd want to have that put in the paper if I'd have been publicly accused of such offenses. It took more than two months after the case was dismissed before a larger newspaper in a neighboring state finally published the story and recounted how the presiding judge had dismissed all charges against Stan.

What concerns me was the way this was handled by the media and by the local townsfolk. The newspaper's criteria for what they considered newsworthy and what is not should caution us whenever we read stories in the press. How many times have you seen allegations in the paper say, "So-and-so was charged with fraud," but you rarely ever see "The charges against So-and-so were all dropped" in a later article? That second article is a rarity. When they are published, they're usually buried deep in the back pages of the paper where most folks seldom journey.

The incident is disappointing on several levels, but it draws to mind how easy it is to forget that the news sources are geared toward the grid of "If it is not news, we're not going to publish it, and if it is news, we're going to broadcast it." They are set up towards that simple model, and thus, those items that they deem as falling into the "not news" category get sidelined, even if it may well change opinions and reputations. This criterion often has to do with what will generate a greater readership. "This is news; therefore, we'll get more readers. That's not news; therefore, we'll see fewer readers," or something along those lines.

This story exposes a problem for recipients of the news, those of us who read and watch press reports and articles, that is becoming a disturbing trend in American society. It may have always been a trend, but it's one that that

I've seen more and more: accusation equals guilt. That attitude shows up often on social media platforms. I, unfortunately, even hear Christians doing the same thing, falling into similar traps. My distant relative faced ostracization and shame in his small town simply because he was accused. Even though all claims against him have been dismissed by the court system, he found that many people in his town will still have nothing more to do with him. I'll have more to say about that trait anon.

The Scheme

This is where my little concept comes into play, my "Master Design" if you will: <u>Validate before you palpitate; authenticate before you propagate</u>. In the area of news articles, broadcasts, and publicized reports, whether by way of standard outlets or through the chatter and gossip of social media, if a specific incident catches your attention, if it causes concern, or alarms you, the first thing to do is <u>validate</u>. I will develop this more in detail as we go along, but for now know that the responsibility that lies with the readers and receivers of news is to make sure we have the facts, and doublecheck the sources.

Especially if an incident gives us an emotional heart attack. So, before you ramp up your heart rate (palpitate), make sure you validate. It's always possible you misread or misheard the account. It's also possible that the incident was misreported.

The second part of the concept simply repeats the first but reminds us of one other aspect. Before we begin sharing a news item with friends, or repeating a story to others (propagate), we must authenticate the specifics and items of the event. Again, it's always possible we have misread or misheard the story, or that the incident was misattributed. By our propagating and spreading what was misread, misheard, or even misreported, we become part of transmitting misinformation.

Obviously, these concepts sound like notions we learned way back in kindergarten. And they probably were. But putting this prime directive into practice, making this concept habitual, is challenging for most people because it means going an extra mile, and learning a new way of digesting news. It really is not that difficult, and I am going to persuade you of this—or make a serious effort to convince you.

I first put together this material for an adult class at my church in 2021. I called that series "Hair on Fire!" I was concerned by what I saw going on during a presidential election season with social media, but also news reports and videos purporting to give "the real truth" about some incident, and so forth. I was, however, most troubled by the distress I saw in the eyes of many Christians, and their reactions to news reports and recorded footage. As a Christian pastor who cares about Christian actions and reactions, what captured my attention was when I observed the way many Christian people simply assumed their favorite news source, venue, tweet, or post put out "the facts" and then watched it impact what they supposed about others, how they responded or reacted toward different people. Very often, too often, accusation equaled guilt. But I also took note of the way several followers of Christ had become disconcerted with growing alarm regarding some national or international incidents they had heard about, but never confirmed.

Therefore, I put together the material for my congregation, thinking it would only constitute two sessions. As I began presenting the lessons, interacting with questions and observations, investigating, etc., the class quickly expanded into five total presentations. I could have gone further than I did but felt I had covered enough for that time. That was one and a half years before I sat down to write this guide, and since then I believe my observations and evaluation have been confirmed manifold times. More studies have surfaced since then, other authors have come to similar conclusions. And further discussions have been had among members of my congregation; discussions around alternative news accounts, media biases and broadcasts, cellphone video recordings that claim to give the unadulterated facts of an incident, broadcasts that misstated details or stated sound bites that are devoid of context, to mention a few examples. Thus, I have had a growing desire to publish what I've learned, and give it to others, in a handy, readable manual.

This book is primarily for Christians of all walks of life. It is written from a Christian perspective, thus, my turning to Sacred Scripture as the ground for how we receive news and how we respond. Pastors, elders, Christian leaders will also be helped. I have seen many of my fellow ministers, in my own denomination and outside, react to unsubstantiated news reports with alarm, or transmit misinformation on several news accounts. I, myself, have done it throughout my years as a Christian leader. It's Paul's injunction to Titus, a Christian minister, that puts extra weight on Christian leaders to lead the way in properly vetting the media: "Show yourself in all respects to be a model of good works, and in your teaching show integrity, dignity, and sound speech that cannot be condemned, so that an opponent may be put to shame, having nothing evil to say about us" (Titus 2:7–8).[4]

Further, what follows in these pages, comes from an American context. Christians in other countries where the media is controlled by their national government have different problems in the area of the media. But, even for them, the principles charted in this book will help them and guide them. They will need to "translate" what the book is discussing for their specific setting.

---

4. Unless otherwise stated, all Scripture quotations are from "The Holy Bible, English Standard Version® (ESV®), Copyright © 2001 by Crossway, a publishing ministry of Good News Publishers. All rights reserved."

The Structure

In this manuscript, one will quickly notice what might be deemed an oddity. At the beginning of each chapter will be the same list of principles. I will highlight the specific tenet covered in that chapter, but all eight concepts will be printed at the head of each chapter. The reason for this redundancy is to help readers (1) see how it all flows together, and (2) increase retention. So, please, resist the temptation to bypass the list, and when you enter each chapter, review the principles afresh.

If a person glances through those eight topics, it should become clear that the book is building as it goes along. Each of the concepts is supported by the previous. This requires that readers be studiously patient. They will need to recognize that many of the questions they will begin to have, while perusing the material, will most likely be answered later in the book.

Further, there will be "practice for the week" suggestions at the end of those chapters that cover the eight ideas. My intention is to inspire readers to rehearse each concept, become familiar with it, and see it work for themselves before they move on to the next. It would be even more helpful if reading/discussion groups took up this book and walked through each chapter together one week at a time. In fact, many of the suggestions are primed for that purpose. And it's in these weekly practice sessions that a reader will often discover the answers to their questions.

Next, I have interspersed five short "interludes" throughout the book, sort of like commercial breaks. These segments are book reviews I have done on select works that are relevant to my overall subject or a specific theme. A version of these book reviews can be found on my blog[5], as well as on Amazon and Goodreads. My ambition for doing this is to show that I'm not alone in my evaluations, to help readers fathom what others have observed, and to arm them with more recommended resources for further study. These breaks or interludes have a slightly different writing style but shouldn't be distracting.

The Scriptures

My desire for this book is to help readers, especially Christian readers, to grow in sensibility and stability as they learn to vet—scrutinize,

---

5. http://mphilliber.blogspot.com/

evaluate, verify—their media intake. This is important because of the directions and guidance of Scripture. As I pointed out in a previous work, "Our Heads on Straight," God wants his people to be sober-minded, reasonable, and right-minded in their actions and relationships. Even when it seems that our world is going out of its mind, we Christians are to be in our right mind. And I can't shake that thesis from my thoughts, and so I have become increasingly attuned to how often sensibility and stability are important traits God intends for us.

To begin, stability is part of God's character which gives us some sure-footedness in a topsy-turvy world: "The LORD is exalted, for he dwells on high; he will fill Zion with justice and righteousness, and he will be the stability of your times, abundance of salvation, wisdom, and knowledge; the fear of the LORD is Zion's treasure" (Isaiah 33:5–6). In the tumultuous context of Isaiah 33, this is good news. God will be the stability of our times when there is economic and societal upheaval. With that gift of stability, he will also be the abundance of our salvation, wisdom, and knowledge. God's stability steadies us.

Additionally, we "who once were alienated and hostile in mind, doing evil deeds, he (Jesus) has now reconciled in his body of flesh by his death, in order to present you holy and blameless and above reproach before him, if indeed you continue in the faith, stable and steadfast, not shifting from the hope of the gospel that you heard" (Colossians 1:21–23). The stable and steady grounding on the gospel, and not shifting from that hope, is the Jesus-centered, Gospel-driven order of the day.

Moreover, James points out that instability is the opposite of what we should be. As he was writing about trusting in God's generous goodness, he encourages us to not slip and slide. "If any of you lacks wisdom, let him ask God, who gives generously to all without reproach, and it will be given him. But let him ask in faith, with no doubting, for the one who doubts is like a wave of the sea that is driven and tossed by the wind. For that person must not suppose that he will receive anything from the Lord; he is a double-minded man, unstable in all his ways" (James 1:5–8). To doubt God's generous goodness is to become a wishy-washy person, like a boat tossed on the waves, and "unstable in all his ways." Instability is being held out as a negative trait, clearly implying that stability is a characteristic we should want to exhibit more and more.

Likewise, Peter, while writing to those "who have obtained a faith of equal standing" with the apostles (2 Peter 1:1), describes false teachers as unstable and spreaders of instability. "There are some things in them that are hard to understand, which the ignorant and unstable twist to their own destruction, as they do the other Scriptures" (3:16b). Therefore, Peter encourages the deeply loved faithful ones to be aware of the destabilizing effects of false teachers and to "take care that you are not carried away with the error of lawless people and lose your own stability" (3:17). Giving heed to the ignorant and unstable can cause us to lose our stability! And part of the way to keep stable is to "grow in the grace and knowledge of our Lord and Savior Jesus Christ" (3:18).

There's more, much more, that can be written in this regard, such as following the quality of steadfastness through Scripture. Or, considering the way self-control surfaces repeatedly in the Bible. And, of course, there's my short book on sober-mindedness I mentioned earlier that would be some help in giving a reader the foundation needed to grow in sensibility and stability.

This whole biblical perspective of practicing sensibility and being a stable people has led a friend of mine to make a helpful observation. Luke H. Davis, who teaches Ethics and Church History at Westminster Christian Academy in St. Louis, states that whether or not "you live in a nation that has free speech, the Bible never guarantees you have that right. God is more interested in your speech and communication being *faithful* than *free*" (Davis 2020, 20). Faithful speech, and being part of the spreading of faithful speech, is integral as we walk with Jesus, who is the way, the truth, and the life (John 14:6). And it is vital as we are filled with the Spirit of truth.

But, even more to the point, growing in sensibility and stability is a chief way to an important end. As the preacher in Ecclesiastes puts it, "Be not quick in your spirit to become angry, for anger lodges in the heart of fools" (Ecclesiastes 7:9). If anger lodges in fools' hearts, especially quick anger, those who don't want to be fools will desire to be free of such hasty heat. In my experience, many North American Christians struggle with hasty heat. But sensibility and stability aid Christians to move beyond outrage.

The next chapter looks into the growing epidemic of outrage infecting many in our churches and communities.

ANGER, ANXIETY, AND AWE

I was talking with him over the phone. He's a fellow military veteran who, because of his chronic ailments, is homebound. Therefore, he depends heavily on electronic media, social media, podcasts, multiple online sources, and phone conversations with friends and relatives to keep in touch with the world and fellow humans. As we were talking, he mentioned that one of his sisters had called him and reported disturbing news. In the environment of Russia's invasion of Ukraine, the ongoing war, and the battle around the Zaporizhzhia Nuclear Power Station, there have also been implied threats of the use of nuclear weapons by the Russians. So, my friend expressed to me that his sister told him, just the day before, that nuclear attack was imminent because the President and the government were issuing iodine tablets to help with radiation fallout. Needless to say, my friend was anxious about the news.

As my friend was recounting this information he had been told, the tone of his voice on the phone alerted me to his concerns. I kept talking with him while I searched published reports online, and quickly noticed that there were no credible sources anywhere saying that the US government was issuing iodine to American citizens. Numerous articles, however, were stating that, as the fighting was going on around the Zaporizhzhia Nuclear Power Station, nations close to that area were issuing iodine tablets to their citizens to protect them in the event of a nuclear leak. I told him what I was reading and that his sister must have misheard the news. The relief in his voice was audible.

There are certain emotions that ramp up our energies so that we become spreaders of stories, news accounts, items of interest, opinions, and so forth. These emotions, when capitalized on, can make us "super-spreaders," contagious propagators that fuel crowd reactions. The larger the infected crowd, then the more transmissible the bigger "We" become; and, the more affected the larger "We" become, the more we spread the disease to even larger crowds. In this present atmosphere of COVID-19 that analogy sticks in my head. I have seen this trend for years and have watched it intensify recently. There are many studies that back up this tendency I have been observing.

Ariel Hasell, a graduate student in the Department of Communication at the University of California, Santa Barbara and Brian E. Weeks, assistant professor in the Department of Communication Studies at the University of Michigan, wrote an article in 2016, entitled "Partisan Provocation: The Role of Partisan News Use and the Emotional Responses in Political Sharing in Social Media." It has been put up on the National Science Foundation's "Human Communication Research" platform. The authors examined the 2012 presidential campaign, and their finding was that "anger remained a significant predictor of information sharing despite a stringent control of previous information sharing behavior ... Of the two negative emotions examined in this study, only anger, not anxiety, was related to campaign information sharing ... We found the pro-attitudinal online news use was related to the respondent's anger directed toward the opposing party's presidential candidate" (Hasell 2016, 650–653). The purpose of the study was to determine what fuels the sharing of information through word-of-mouth, including social media and so forth. One of the strong emotions they found was anger. People would get angry and what they were angry about is what they would spread the most.⁂

Another study, "Anger, Fear, and Echo Chambers: The Emotional Basis for Online Behavior" was published by researchers from the Institute for Social Research and the University of Oslo in Norway. To summarize the work of Dag Wollebæk, Rune Karlsen, Kari Steen-Johnsen, and Bernard Enjolras, they found that anger and anxiety were good predictors of social media involvement, trench warfare, and echo chamber dynamics. Anger would often lead participants to seek out and find news sources and information that confirmed their position, whereas others who were anxious would actually broaden out their searches and investigations to include those who might disagree (Wollebæk, et al. 2019).

Even in the areas of marketing and advertising, this recognition is getting some notice.

Jonah Berger, Joseph G. Campbell Assistant Professor of Marketing, and Katherine L. Milkman, Assistant Professor of Operations and Information Management, both at the Wharton School of the University of Pennsylvania, penned "What Makes Online Content Viral?" For this report, the authors completed three studies, one of which examined 7,000 articles from the *New York Times* in a three-month period (Berger and Milkman 2012). Their aim was to see which articles were emailed by people the most. The authors found that "more positive content is more viral." Further, "Importantly, however, our findings also reveal that virality is driven by more than just valence[6]. Sadness, anger, and anxiety are all negative emotions, but while sadder content is less viral, content that evokes more anxiety or anger is actually more viral." The more anxious or angry, the more likely it will fuel what people share. To put it in Berger's words when he was interviewed by the *Smithsonian Magazine*, "Anger is a high-arousal emotion, which drives people to take action. It makes you feel fired up, which

6. *Valence* is a term used in Psychology to denote a one-dimensional value assigned to something that can be positive or negative.

makes you more likely to pass things on" (Shaer 2014).

This leads Berger and Milkman to explain to marketers how important high-arousal emotions are if they want their ad campaigns to become infectious. "Our findings also shed light on how to design successful viral marketing campaigns and craft contagious content. While marketers often produce content that paints their product in a positive light, our results suggest that content will be more likely to be shared if it evokes high-arousal emotions. Advertisements that make consumers content or relaxed, for example, will not be as viral as those that amuse them. Furthermore, while some marketers might shy away from advertisements that evoke negative emotions, our results suggest that negative emotion can actually increase transmission if it is characterized by activation" (Berger and Milkman 2012).

Anger and anxiety are strong indicators of what sells and what gets shared. There was, though, a surprising twist to this study. One of the trends they noticed is that awe, "the emotion of self-transcendence, a feeling of admiration and elevation in the face of something greater than the self" stoked the feelings of wonder and excitement and had an equal or greater influence on what was broadcast (Ibid.). As Berger observed when interviewed by Smithsonian Magazine, "Awe gets our hearts racing and our blood pumping. This increases the desire for emotional connection and drives us to share" (Shaer 2014).

Unfortunately, what is most noticeable is that broadcasting awe is not our normal experience. Rather, anger and anxiety seem to be what one meets the most. High-arousal emotions that are easy to stir up, whether by headlines, newscasts, social media feeds, blogs, podcasts, or gossip, drive most of our media consumption and diffusion, as well as our opinions and actions. This has become so much the case that our present social ecosystem could easily be described as the *outrage culture*.

As Berger and Milkman point out to marketers, "Negative emotion can actually increase transmission if it is characterized by activation," which means that anger, or outrage, is one of those high-octane emotions that activate us, get us to move, vote, purchase, join, pay attention, gab, etc. Outrage is potent in what gets broadcast. Outrage is infectious.

For example, on social media, outrage "sells." It feels good, and it makes us feel good toward ourselves. Justin Tosi, Assistant Professor of Philosophy at Texas Tech University, and Brandon Warmke, Assistant Professor of Philosophy at Bowling Green State University, make this crystal clear when they write, "One reason people express moral outrage is to alleviate their own guilt … when people feel complicit in moral wrongdoing, they try to alleviate this guilt and protect their images of themselves as good people. They do this by turning to outrage and punitive attitudes toward others. Once expressed, outrage makes them feel morally good once again" (Tosi and Warmke 2020, 60–61).

The connection between high-arousal emotions, grandstanding, and profitability come together in the words of Shane Parrish, a one-time cybersecurity expert for a top Canadian intelligence agency. Parrish observes, "Modern media treats outrage as a profitable commodity. This often takes the form of articles which attribute malice to that which could be explained by incompetence or ignorance. We see examples of this play out in the media multiple times a day. People rush to take offense at anything which contradicts their worldview or which they imagine to do so. Media outlets are becoming increasingly skilled at generating assumptions of malicious intent" (Parrish 2017). Outrage sells. Outrage pays off. Outrage makes us easy marks.

Dan Crenshaw, a medically retired Navy Seal and US Representative, takes note of this trend as well. He observes,

> "Passion successfully overrides reason and accomplishment. Who gets more attention, the public figure who calmly sees both sides of an argument or a perceived grievance and tries to mediate, or an activist who angrily marches down the street proclaiming their righteousness? . . . Our outrage culture is increasingly drawn to voices perceived as authentic, which is usually just another code for excessive emotion. Thoughtful

argument is downgraded while fist-shaking activism is rewarded. There is an assumption that anger must be connected to righteousness. Passion replaces reason. Attitude—owning the libs or the cons—replaces sophisticated argument" (Crenshaw 2020, 58–59).

Anger, outrage, anxiety. Why point out all these studies and statements? Because they help us to diagnose the disease that is sickening us. The atmosphere we inhale is charged with the miasma of outrage, which means we breath it in, soak it in, drink it in. Then it spews forth from our own hearts, heads, and mouths. It infects our marriages, politics, school board meetings, denominations, and churches. One can't miss its symptoms on social media or news reports. Outrage sells. Outrage is profitable. Outrage has an emotional payoff. Outrage makes us an easy mark.

But inevitably, someone will say, "Righteous outrage is right! It's biblical, preacher! Don't you know that Jesus was outraged when he went into the temple and overturned tables and drove out the money changers!" Yes, you are correct. "Don't you know that Moses was outraged when he came down the mountain and saw God's people worshiping a recently made golden calf, and he dashed the stone tablets with the Ten Commandments written by the finger of God!" Again, you are correct. "Don't you know that Jesus will return one day to tread the winepress of the fury of the wrath of God the Almighty" (Revelation 19:15). Once more, I heartily affirm that you are correct.

Our problem is that we are too easily outraged, too quickly stirred up to anger. We're more like Saul of Tarsus, ready to breath out threats and murder against others (Acts 9:1), to display zeal for God by "binding and delivering to prison both men and women" (Acts 22:4). And these fits of anger Paul will later describe as "works of the flesh," and "those who do such things will not inherit the kingdom of God" (Galatians 5:19–21).

Back in the day when chain emails used to be trendy, I received one from someone close to me. She forwarded me an email purporting that President Obama had signed an Executive

Order that financed Hamas. The email even listed the Executive Order number. The point of the email was to get recipients like me to become angry so we would act, sending letters and emails to Senators and to the White House protesting such abhorrent evil.

Instead of being roused to angry protest, I researched the Executive Order. What I found was that the President had simply signed into execution that our country was to send something like $200,000 to fund Palestinian secondary education and elementary schools. It was the same Executive Order signed by his predecessors, President George W. Bush, President Bill Clinton, and President George W.H. Bush. Now, I might disagree with this policy and think it a poor use of our national funds and an even poorer international policy. It wasn't, however, the horrendous evil it was made out to be.

I sent these facts to my dear one who had sent me the chain email, with the Executive Order link to the White House. I then pointed out that as Christians we still have a weighty obligation to follow the ninth commandment and not bear false witness. Even if we wanted such actions to be true of a president we disagreed with, so we could have reasons to validate our distrust, it didn't give us license to propagate false information. Unfortunately, my response was not well received. Outrage sells, and outrage makes us an easy mark.

Yet, outrage as a display of the works of the flesh and truly righteous anger is hard to differentiate, especially since we are all self-justifying people. We too easily vindicate our actions or excuse them. So, anytime we flare up it feeds our sense of moral rectitude as "more righteous than those people!" As Crenshaw was working hard to get us to see, outrage is perceived as authentic. That thought should make us pause and reflect and slow down.

In fact, Scripture is replete with warnings about being incensed and inflamed too quickly. Take a walk through the biblical book of Proverbs, for example, and note every time anger is addressed. It doesn't take long to recognize ourselves on the problematic side of those verses— if we have any humility and self-awareness. For example, "Whoever is slow to anger has great understanding, but he who has a hasty temper exalts folly" (Proverbs 14:29). "A hot-tempered man stirs up strife, but he who is slow to anger quiets contention" (Proverbs 15:18). "Whoever is slow to anger is better than the mighty, and he who rules his spirit than he who takes a city" (Proverbs 16:32).

What, then, should be our aim? Clearly, there are places for fitting outrage. But exhibiting too much anger, too quickly, too loudly, and too publicly, numbs us and anaesthetizes those around us. Then, when we really do stumble onto valid reasons to become angry—like a child being molested, or a black man being dragged through the streets and lynched—few will pay attention. They will likely hear it as nothing more than deafening noise arising from our cultural outrage.

A good way to summarize most of the concerns in this chapter is in the words of Jonathan Dodson. He is pastor of City Life Church in Austin, Texas, who wrote a book about overcoming moral chaos by way of the Beatitudes. He stated that, "If we believe self-expression is our greatest right, we'll rarely exercise restraint. In fact, anger is the emotion most easily spread across social media" (Dodson 2020, 131).

Instead of self-expression and spreading anger, by the help of God, by the working of his Holy Spirit, and by the blessing of Christ, we should want to move beyond outrage. As Paul describes things once he has finished talking about the works of the flesh:

"But the fruit of the Spirit is love, joy, peace, patience, kindness, goodness, faithfulness, gentleness, self-control; against such things there is no law. And those who belong to Christ Jesus have crucified the flesh with its passions and desires. If we live by the Spirit, let us also keep in step with the Spirit. Let us not become conceited, provoking one another, envying one another." (Galatians 5:22–26)

The aim of this book, then, is what I stated in the introduction. To grow in sensibility and stability so that we can move beyond outrage. Toward that end come the important principles in the following chapters.

Practice for the Week:

- Whether it's a tweet or Instagram post or news article, check yourself. If you find yourself being hastily motivated to despair or to deploy snide comments publicly, see if anger or anxiety is the emotion swelling up in you. Take note of it, and then start logging how often anger-inducing or anxiety-provoking articles and posts catch your attention and suck you in. After three to five days, tell your book study group, or a friend, what you discovered.

- While watching a newscast, or taking in some other news accounts, when you find any high-arousal emotions ramping up in you, take a break. Stop and step back. Go outside and allow the breeze to run over you. Spend some time praying that the Sovereign God would take note of what you just read or saw or heard, and guide you toward a healthy, holy, godly response. Or that he would make it clear to you that no response is necessary.

- Look for reports and news sources that recount awe, wonder, excitement, and admiration. Maybe it's about a person's heroic actions in the face of severe adversity, or an unfiltered photo of some natural wonder. Once you find two or three of those accounts, consider why they are so significant. If they inspire you to lift

up your heart in thanksgiving and grati-
tude, then do so.

MICHAEL W. PHILLIBER

ACCUSATION DOES NOT MEAN GUILT

Accusation Does Not Mean Guilt
Guilty until Proven Innocent?
Suspend Judgment
Hanlon's Razor
Human Reporters
Reasonable Explanations
Media Angle
Over-Reporting

It was the summer of 2020. Emmanuel Cafferty, a Mexican American, worked for a San Diego power company and had just spent a long day mapping utility lines. He was headed home in his company pickup truck with its logo on the side, his window down, and his arm casually dangling out the window. Not too many miles away from his route home there was a Black Lives Matter rally. As he was travelling home, someone pulled up next to him and gave him an "Okay" hand signal. The one where the index finger and thumb connect for a circle and the remaining fingers sort of stick out on their own. Cafferty casually flashed the sign back to the other driver. As he was giving the sign, the driver of the other vehicle took his picture and then took off. Little did Cafferty know this brief incident would change his life.

Two hours after the episode Cafferty received a call from his supervisor who notified him his picture had been posted on Twitter with him giving a white supremacist sign. Several people had called the company demanding he be dismissed. He lost his job, was vilified through social media, and has had his life turned upside down (MacDonald 2021). He is the victim of an accusation that, for many, equals guilt. Where there is no due process, no trial outside the court of public opinion, no appellate review system. There was a picture, a media venue, and an accusation. Then comes the flash-bang and his livelihood is up in smoke.

That concept is a hard pill to swallow if someone is on the receiving end. But it seems to be that this is the model many media receivers and social media users follow. In my experience, accusation equaling guilt has been around for quite some time. Probably since as far back as Genesis 3. But I have noticed that the trend of taking up this perspective, and acting out on it, looks to be on the rise and is usually attended with a lot of heat and vitriol. So let me briefly define my terms.

Accusation is where someone alleges a person did wrong, whether it was a criminal act, a moral failure, or a violation of new social standards. The type of accusation I'm thinking of, however, is the kind that is videoed, photographed, recorded, or written up in a news report or dispatched through Internet platforms. Guilt, therefore, is assumed by the court of public opinion based on nothing more than the accusation. There is no trial, no investigation, but one is simply accused, which leads to being condemned as guilty by the crowd.

For example, in May 2017, at the Putney Bridge in London. A bus camera recorded the moment where a jogger passed by a woman and shoved her into the path of the bus. After a time, the police released the video, which went viral (spread over social media sites as well as other broadcasts). An American, Eric Bellquist, a partner at the Mayfair-based private equity firm, was accused of being the Putney Bridge Pusher. He was quickly arrested and taken to be questioned by the Met Police. Even though he had proof he was in the United States at the time of the incident (which caused the police to release him), the accusation, having been made public along with the video, brought him quite a bit of grief, including death threats. It got to the point where he had to hire personal security for his own protection. Accusation equals guilt, or at least, that is how many receive, reason, and react to news and online reports. It is all assumed without any further reflection.

To have, and to act on, the supposition that to be accused means one is guilty creates a freight train load of social difficulties. It underlies most of our anger and rage that swells up, fueling suspicion and incivility. It also fosters our fears and anxieties. As Douglas S. Bursch, a Christian minister who is a former newspaper columnist and onetime talk radio host, describes it, our "online existence is turning us into angry, dehumanizing, polarizing people" (Bursch 2021, 2).

To put things in a different light, when a person takes on the assumption that accusation signifies guilt, they then believe that they have a right to assume the accused is guilty. This leads many to think they have a right to act on this assumption of guilt. All of this is part of prioritizing the sovereign self. Alan Noble, Assistant Professor of English at Oklahoma Baptist University in Shawnee, Oklahoma, makes this helpful observation when he writes, "Outside of a culture of virtue grounded in an external source, science, technology, and the market have been driven to produce a society that prioritizes the sovereign individual" (Noble 2018, 3). In prioritizing the sovereign self, the sovereign individual, one becomes judge, jury, and executioner because he or she is entitled to such an all-encompassing authority.

Not only is the concept of accusation equaling guilt a central flaw this book is addressing, but it is also a significant fault spoken against in Scripture.

There's a reason the Bible, from deep in the Hebrew Scriptures all the way into the bowels of the New Testament, requires that an accusation be confirmed at the mouth of two or three witnesses. "A single witness shall not suffice against a person for any crime or for any wrong in connection with any offense that he has committed. Only on the evidence of two witnesses or of three witnesses shall a charge be established" (Deuteronomy 19:15). "Do not admit a charge against an elder except on the evidence of two or three witnesses" (1 Timothy 5:19). It helps to stop people from assuming that accusation inevitably indicates guilt.

Yet, even in the face of two or three witnesses, Scripture is clear that the truth can still be mangled, "If a malicious witness arises to accuse a person of wrongdoing, then both parties to the dispute shall appear before the LORD, before the priests and the judges who are in office in those days. The judges shall inquire diligently, and if the witness is a false witness and has accused his brother falsely, then you shall do to him as he had meant to do to his brother. So you shall purge the evil from your midst" (Deuteronomy 19:16–19). As God is coaching and guiding his people in this passage, he wants us to take a slower, more reflective, and thoughtful approach that doesn't jump to conclusions. It's possible that the indictment is erroneous. And it's also possible that the visual, photographed, recorded "evidence" might be fallacious or misleading. We need to cool our jets, as my parents used to say, and slow down.

Further, not routinely jumping to the conclusion that an allegation means a person is guilty is an important trait of wholesome, godly wisdom. For example, "If one gives an answer before he hears, it is his folly and shame" (Proverbs 18:13). "An intelligent heart acquires knowledge, and the ear of the wise seeks knowledge" (Proverbs 18:15). "The one who states his case first seems right, until the other comes and examines him" (Proverbs 18:17). "Death and life are in the power of the tongue, and those who love it will eat its fruits" (Proverbs 18:21).

There are several sensible reasons for us not to immediately assume the worst. Just because a cellphone video purportedly shows a person committing a crime, or a news article records a person being indicted for lawbreaking, or co-workers censuring a colleague for what they think are racist sentiments, does not make it so. Those charges may turn out to be true, but to instantaneously suppose they are goes well beyond sensibleness and wisdom. It definitely breaks through the wholesome boundaries God has given us.

The first positive principle to take with us is to realize accusation means only accusation. When we see a video on our online platforms alleging that a person has committed some crime or social offense, or moral failure, it is still purely an allegation. When a news piece surfaces that accuses a person or a candidate or a politician of some evil action, it is still only a claim not a certainty of culpability. For Christians, Scripture is very clear that instead of being like our society, we need to slow down, take up a reasonable perspective, and not follow the mob toward the local lynching. As Ben Sasse, US Senator from Nebraska, warns, "All of us are susceptible to the mindless self-righteousness of the Twitter mob, absolutely certain that we're on the 'right side of history' on every issue, no matter how small" (Sasse 2018, 151). If we slow down and keep in mind that accusation only means accusation, then it will help us to learn to <u>validate before we palpitate and authenticate before we propagate</u>.

Recently, I was called upon to do the graveside and funeral of one of my parishioners, Tom Daxon. Tom had been elected Oklahoma State Auditor and Inspector in 1978 and also served as the Oklahoma Secretary of Finance and Revenue. He was a significant catalyst in the convictions in the 1980s county commissioners' scandal in Oklahoma.[7] A man of resilience, integrity, and faith. As I stood at the graveside, I noticed his family headstone that stands above his grave. The motto etched into the granite puts the point of this chapter in a succinct way:

"IN GOD WE TRUST
ALL OTHERS WE AUDIT"

That summarizes the scriptural perspective that undergirds this chapter. Accusation does not equal guilt, so audit the accusations, audit the news report charges, audit the video allegations before you jump on the guilt bandwagon.

Where would Emmanuel Cafferty be now if people who saw that picture of him online had simply stopped and recognized that accusation means accusation, and it doesn't indicate guilt? If we make a habit of assuming the worst, if we keep on thinking that accusation most certainly means guilt, then the next step will be to

7. To read more about Tom Daxon and his life, there's a fair and well-done page on him in Wikipedia: https://en.wikipedia.org/wiki/Tom_Daxon

accept the notion that the indicted is guilty until proven innocent. And that is the subject of the next chapter.

Practice for the Week:

- This week, attempt to read your media sources through the lens that accusation does not equal guilt. If you need, stop partway through the post or article and say out loud, "Okay, Mike, accusation doesn't mean guilt. Accusation only means accusation."

- Take up a notepad and start documenting how many tweets, posts, and articles make allegations about someone or some group. Then look for any language in that source that seems to want readers to assume the named people or parties are guilty.

- At the end of the week, reflect on your own mental temperature. Has this exercise altered your heart rate? Hopefully, you'll notice that you're processing media reports in a much calmer state.

GUILTY UNTIL PROVEN INNOCENT?

Accusation Does Not Mean Guilt
Guilty until Proven Innocent?
Suspend Judgment
Hanlon's Razor
Human Reporters
Reasonable Explanations
Media Angle
Over-Reporting

When I was a young boy living in Moore, Oklahoma (Oklahoma's tornado magnet, or so it seemed), in the early 1970s, I was attending a brand-new school. It was one of those new-fangled educational fad establishments. Well, something happened in the class, and I was involved. I can't recall what details were included but I wasn't in any trouble, for once. Whatever transpired, I was excited to tell my dad about it. When he returned home that evening, I started babbling on about what had occurred and mentioned how I spoke to the teacher regarding whatever it was. My dad misheard me and thought I was telling him I had mouthed off to the teacher and had gotten in trouble. So, he promptly snatched me up, marched me into my bedroom, made me bend over, and proceeded to spank me with his leather belt (fear not, dear reader, I am no worse for the wear). Once I had finished crying and wiping my eyes, my father said, "Now, son, tell me what happened again." I told him and he listened carefully. Suddenly, his face went stunned blank. He stopped me and asked, "So, you didn't mouth off to the teacher and you didn't get in trouble?" "No, dad. This is what I told her, and this is what happened." "Okay, son, you didn't mouth off, and you didn't get in trouble?" "No sir," I replied. He slowly shook his head, gathered me up in his arms, and profusely apologized for having misheard me and having spanked me. He even asked me to forgive him. It was a memorable moment filled with deep life lessons about the humanness of parents, what forgiveness feels like, and real love.

I tell this story because it's an illustration of what happens when one is assumed guilty until proven innocent. Dad assumed I was guilty (and I'll simply say, my life patterns gave him good reason to immediately go there) and thus, he "heard" and acted on that assumption of my guilt. Thankfully, in that situation I was proven innocent, but many times one who has been assumed to be guilty never gets the opportunity to prove their innocence. It's almost as if the attitude is, "They're guilty until proven innocent, and—*dag gummit*—they'll never be proven innocent!"

It all fits together. If in some people's minds accusation means that the accused is guilty, then it's just a short step into "and guilty until proven innocent." And proving one's innocence when guilt is assumed is like pushing a rock uphill while others are pushing downhill from the other side. If you've ever been on the receiving end of a situation like this, you know how helpless it makes one feel. Anything you say can and will be used against you in the court of public opinion to prove you're still guilty.

Guilty until proven innocent is humorously acted out in *Monty Python and the Holy Grail*, in the scene of the witch's trial[8]. The peasants race up to Sir Bedevere, dragging along a woman and crying out, "We have found a witch! Burn her! burn her!" Then one of the peasants states, "We have found a witch, may we burn her?" When Sir Bedevere asks how they know she's a witch, the reply is, "She looks like one!" The woman accused of being a witch energetically retorts that she's not a witch. Sir Bedevere points out that she's dressed like a witch, and the woman describes how the peasants dressed her up like one, even giving her a fake witch's nose, among other hagridden ornaments. The conversation begins to drift into how one can tell if the woman is a witch, and spirals down into witches being made of wood that floats and is the same weight as a duck. The ending of that scene takes a funny twist, but for our purposes, this is what guilty until proven innocent looks like. So certain that the woman is a witch, the villagers see everything as proof of her guilt, and when that proof is lacking, they dress her up as one. After the viewer gets over the comicalness of this scene, and stops to reflect, it becomes quite

8. One can easily find this scene online with a search of "Monty Python and the Witch's Trial."

easy to spot the many ways this works out in our daily media intake and relationships.

The presumption of guilt in the legal sphere is officially verboten[9]. I have been in plenty of jury pools and sat through the selection process enough times to know that our court systems are very concerned to do what they reasonably can to head off the presumption of guilt among potential jurors. If I were being tried as a suspect, it's exactly what I hope I would face. To have a jury of my peers who are not gauging how guilty I am. Rather, that they would be thinking that I might be innocent, and the prosecution must prove otherwise, beyond a reasonable doubt.

Interesting enough, that is where Scripture wants us to be: assume innocence, unless proven guilty. I go back to the biblical passages we read in the previous chapter. In those passages, God has set up the need for more than one witness to establish a charge against the accused because a person is not to be considered guilty, but innocent, unless proven otherwise. "A single witness shall not suffice against a person for

9. German for "forbidden." The generation surfacing after the Second World War used this word enough that I heard my grandmother apply it many times.

any crime or for any wrong in connection with any offense that he has committed. Only on the evidence of two witnesses or of three witnesses shall a charge be established" (Deuteronomy 19:15. See also Deuteronomy 17:6–7). The fact that Yahweh prescribes the need to have witnesses, and not to be satisfied with only one accusing voice, is profound. God wants us to assume innocence first, in the face of accusations.

This is why we're to apply this very approach in more personal settings, such as with our neighbors. "If one gives an answer before he hears, it is his folly and shame" (Proverbs 18:13). "An intelligent heart acquires knowledge, and the ear of the wise seeks knowledge" (Proverbs 18:15). "The one who states his case first seems right, until the other comes and examines him" (Proverbs 18:17). In fact, Proverbs 18:17 is dripping with situational awareness[10]. We're to take a "wait-and-see" approach, to assume "there may be far more to this story than meets the eye" whenever anyone—reporters, tweets, posts, or people—rush up to us to make their case, declaring how they're right and the other party is wrong.

---

10. *Situational awareness* comes from my law enforcement and martial arts background. Being aware of the bigger picture, instead of being trapped in a tunnel vision that zooms down to "this" event and blacks out the surrounding context.

Not only have I found the biblical wisdom in Proverbs 18:17 helpful in pastoral circumstances, it has also become a working principle as I ingest news reports, online indictments, and watch videos purporting to give the "real" truth about this event or that individual or those people. I know from personal experience that it's too easy to lose sight of the larger context and assume this individual sitting in front of me is giving me all the facts. The reality is that they are normally giving me the truth, as they see it or as it fits their perception of the moment. And with a little investigation, or a bit of listening to others, it becomes quickly clear that there's more to the story that often changes the whole event. This translates over to news sources, and into our Internet declarations.

Proverbs 18:13 should drench our perspectives, "If one gives an answer before he hears, it is his folly and shame." Taking a slower, assumption-of-innocence approach to broadcasts, newsflashes, indictments, and denunciations includes being slower to answer, giving oneself a longer fuse, not hastily jumping into outrage mode, until you accumulate more details. And one way to give your heart space, before you quickly declare another's guilt, is to make "the best possible case for the alternative position prior to offering a response" (Gibson and Beitler 2020, 114). To frame the other person's position fairly and justly means you force yourself to hear what they're really saying or writing or propagating.

And, in the case of someone being accused of some offense by others, this will mean you will think through their defense as if you were the one being accused. This will compel you to gather more facts and specifics. It obliges you to turn down the hurry and drop the temperature and think through (1) what factually happened if it's possible to discover, and (2) what likely happened. To follow this way aids you in hearing, so that you don't step in a warm pile of folly and shame and raise some unnecessary stink.

To go a step further, our Lord was clear about the texture of our engagements with others. These are statements that often get misused, but it's worth hearing and reading them. "Be merciful, even as your Father is merciful. Judge not, and you will not be judged; condemn not, and you will not be condemned; forgive, and you will be forgiven; give, and it will be given to you. Good measure, pressed down, shaken together, running over, will be put into your lap. For with the measure you use it will be measured back to you" (Luke 6:36–38). It's that last line that tells us how we're to grasp what Jesus is saying. Jesus is not talking about some divine–human quid pro quo, this-for-that. Instead, the context is how we deal with people as we live daily with others; "with the measure you use it will be measured back to you."

The point of Jesus' statement is this: Be as charitable and generous and gracious to others as you want others to be toward you. Therefore, when you're accused, you would want your family, friends, coworkers, neighbors, media reporters, Facebook pundits, and fellow church members to consider you innocent until proven guilty. And that same biblical ethic is how we are expected to treat others. Instead of assuming guilt, we take a position that starts with, "He/she is innocent until shown otherwise." I don't care how many podcasters, YouTubers, tweeters, or others scream and shout "We've found a witch! May we burn her?" or its equivalent. The biblical starting point is from a disposition of assuming the accused's innocence.

This is another part of <u>validating before palpitating and authenticating before propagating</u>.

To assume innocence rather than guilt, until shown otherwise, means we will suspend judgment. That's where we go when we come to the next trait. But first, we need to take a break and think about humility.

Practice for the Week:

- Take this week to read through several news pieces where crimes or violations of social codes are reported. Observe the language used and see if it is urging readers to immediately assume that the persons reported on are guilty before there's any investigation or trial.

- Scroll through your news feeds and social media notifications, watching for the writer's assumption that this group or that individual they are talking about is guilty. See if they use specific verbal tools to get readers to jump on the "guilty until proven innocent" bandwagon. Maybe it's highly emotional language or "righteous" assertions without proven evidence.

- While reading through your sources, stop partway, take a deep breath, and remind yourself that the proper, biblical approach is to consider that the accused is innocent until proven guilty.
- When reading a savory post condemning someone of immorality, treason, or some such, stop and ask yourself, "Do I want this to be true because I don't like this person or group?"
- Using your notepad, make notes on what you've been finding all week.

INTERLUDE: HUMILITY

"God resists the proud, but gives grace to the humble," and synonymous statements, echo through Scripture from Genesis to Revelation. It shows up in Proverbs, comes forth from the lips of Jesus, spills onto the page in James and 1 Peter, and even floats to the surface in Revelation. Humility is an important subject, and a difficult quality. Christopher Hutchinson, Senior Pastor of Grace Covenant Presbyterian Church in Blacksburg, Virginia, has given us some help in thinking about the virtue of humility in his 252-page paperback, *Rediscovering Humility: Why the Way up Is Down*. This volume is an easy-to-read, devotional approach that is friendly and thoughtful, and meant to be useful for most anyone.

Hutchinson spends three chapters introducing humility, and then allows faith, hope, and love to guide the rest of the discussion. His tactic is exegetical, theological, pastoral, and devotional. *Rediscovering Humility* is chock-full of timely quotations from puritans and pastors, and swimming in stories. The author mainly hopes "that this little work will jump-start a dialogue on what humility should look like in today's church" (Hutchinson 2018, xviii). I think his book may well do just that.

In *Rediscovering Humility*, the author doesn't shy away from important topics. Not only does the book touch on sin, salvation, sanctification, celebration, and the celestial, but it sagaciously and solicitously comes at other subjects as well. To give the reader a taste of the dishes Hutchinson serves up, here are several short samples. Regarding theology and doctrine, "Christians are not claiming that they have discovered the truth themselves, but that a gracious God has revealed it to them . . . Closely connected to the idea of resting in Christ's accomplished work is the dictum of healthy self-doubt" (49–50). In the area of social justice, the author reminds us that the "New Testament, however, is not interested in upending social structures as a whole . . . The gospel has come to do greater things than to restructure current social structures" (118). Hutchinson encourages churches to lean more heavily on prayer, because a "church that does not pray much does not sense its need for God's grace much" (135). When focusing on Christian leadership, the author rightly asserts that authentic "Christian leadership needs to be relentlessly meek—consistently and self-consciously humble in all its endeavors after the model of Christ. Indeed, humility is the goal of all true Christian leadership" (144). As the author addresses unity, he notes that "God's grace in the gospel creates a gospel-wrought humility, which, in turn, leads to a gospel-driven unity" (180). And, while discussing church well-being, the author observes that "when churches are self-focused, all about their own growth and branding, then there is no rest there for God's people, no gospel. The churches have become factories, when the world needs a garden—a place to rest in Christ from one's own works, surrounded only by His beauty and grace" (213).

There was one remarkably gracious and wise consideration that Hutchinson made in the area of racism and remembering past generations. I am compelled to quote it in full:

> "Regarding the past, believers may look with horror upon the

sins of slavery and Jim Crow, and rightly condemn both institutions. But do they really think that many believers today would have avoided the cultural pressures that captured so much of the church at that time? Would most of today's white Christians really have been among that small, persecuted minority in the antebellum American South who actively opposed slavery?... When today's believers evaluate the sins of past generations, humility and empathy are always in good order, even as we speak the truth and hold to the standards of God's Word. Christians might also consider what future generations will say about today's church when believers look back at our cultural accommodations. All have sinned and fall short of the glory of God." (204–205)

Humility should affect our judgments of the past.

Rediscovering Humility ends with a list of one hundred verses on humility, and an index of scriptural references. Both of those will make the book usable for preachers and Bible teachers. If a topical index had been added, this volume would have been even more helpful.

All told, *Rediscovering Humility* is the right book to read as one thinks about the introduction to this book and the last three chapters. Humility aids us in seeing our susceptibility to being played by anger and anxiety. Humility gives us the meekness to recognize our own fault in immediately assuming that because a person was accused, then they're guilty. Humility is deeply needed to slow us down and restrain us from falling over the cliff of "guilty until proven innocent." Since humility gives us a healthy dose of self-doubt, it aids us in trusting God, and making sure we audit all others. *Rediscovering Humility* should be snatched up in bulk and handed out. It's a book I happily recommend to all, especially my fellow ministers.

And now we return to our broadcast.

MICHAEL W. PHILLIBER

SUSPEND JUDGMENT

Accusation Does Not Mean Guilt
Guilty until Proven Innocent?
Suspend Judgment
Hanlon's Razor
Human Reporters
Reasonable Explanations
Media Angle
Over-Reporting

Remember those old black-and-white Westerns? Maybe the *Rifleman* or *Rawhide* or *The Defiant Ones*. Inevitably, in the story line, there would be an accusation made about someone cattle rustling or horse thieving. Then a posse would be rounded up, the accused would be captured and, if he was lucky, he would be hauled back into town for the marshal to lock up. Later, maybe after too much time at the saloon, or for whatever reason, a talking head would rise up above the crowd, get the folks roused and hot, and then convince them that

"We need to string up that filthy varmint!" That's when the raging mob, filled with citizens who would normally be decent folk, would gather in an angry pack, move as a crowd to the jail, and everything would get nasty at that point. Sometimes a respectable sheriff might talk the people off the ledge, at other times the crush of people overwhelmed the sheriff and dragged the accused outside and ended his life.

That's the kind of thing that happened in Greenville South Carolina to Willie Earle back in 1947. Earle, a twenty-four-year-old black cab driver, was accused on circumstantial evidence of robbing and stabbing to death Thomas Brown, a white cab driver, and was arrested and charged with Brown's death. The next evening, on 16 February 1947, a motorcade of taxi drivers drove to the jail, forced their way in, grabbed Earle, and then hauled him off to beat, stab, and shoot him to death. Besides the significant underlying ethnic issues, the trouble was that the allegation that Earle had killed Brown meant to the crowd that he was guilty, and therefore, they held him guilty until proven innocent, something he would never be allowed to have the opportunity to do.

A similar event occurred earlier on the 24th of May in 1911 just outside Okemah, Oklahoma, the Okfuskee County seat. This is the town where the folk singer Woody Guthrie would be born and grow up. The reports of what exactly happened are conflicting, but on the 2nd of May Deputy Sheriff George Loney was fatally shot while serving a search warrant to look for a stolen cow. Laura Nelson, a black woman, and her thirteen-year-old son, L.D., were at the house. While the Deputy and his men were searching the property, Laura tried to take a rifle from her son. One report says she got the weapon free, loaded it, and shot the Deputy in cold blood. Another report states that a struggle ensued between mother, son, and the Deputy, when the rifle went off. In either case, Deputy Loney was struck in the abdomen by the bullet, walked outside, and bled to death. Laura and L.D. were arrested and taken to Okemah.

Mother and son stood before the judge on the 10th of May, where they were officially charged with murder and held without bail in the Okfuskee County Jail in Okemah to await trial. Then, the night before their arraignment to answer the charges, several men gathered a mob who broke into the jail and forcefully hauled Laura and L.D. from the cell. They took them to an old bridge over the Canadian River and hanged them. Even a local photographer took pictures of the crowd of onlookers on the bridge, with the two victims still hanging there, and turned the pictures into postcards. Years later, Woody Guthrie, haunted by this story and the postcards he saw still being sold in his hometown, wrote the haunting folk song, "Don't Kill My Baby and My Son."

Beyond the ethnically driven problems behind the mob lynching of both Willie Earl and Laura and L.D. Nelson, there is an even greater issue: Justice. In neither case was genuine justice served. In the case of Willie Earl, it was never proved who killed Thomas Brown. If Earl didn't do it, then the real murderer escaped notice. In the case of the Nelsons, murder was never proven, and never given the opportunity to be confirmed. In both cases accusation equaled guilt, and so they were guilty until proven innocent. But an even more sinister aspect of both situations is that a mob was roused, with no evidence, where there was no opportunity to cross-examine witnesses, and there was no recognition that there could be more to the story. Mobs were aroused to shovel out violence and bloody power to promote the pack's moral uprightness and virtue.

We quickly cringe when we read such reports, most of the time thinking that we're above such mindless vigilantism. But the reality is that humans, created as social creatures, are easily moved as a herd. It doesn't take much to arouse masses to move together and "hang" people. It happens too often on social media. A person will post an incriminating accusation and, before long, that post will gather a large number of people who comment and share the post. It becomes contagious and spreads like a bad virus drawing more and more heat. Emmanuel Cafferty, the Mexican American I mentioned in a previous chapter, felt the effects of "mob lynching." Many others on the right and on the left of the political/social spectrum have undergone the virtual rope dropped around their necks as well.

This tendency toward mob rule was a concern for some of the American founders. James Madison, in Federalist Paper Number 10, spoke of this when he decried the rise of factions, "By a faction, I understand a number of citizens, whether amounting to a majority or a minority of the whole, who are united and actuated by some common impulse of passion, or of interest, adverse to the rights of other citizens, or to the permanent and aggregate interests of the community" (Hamilton, Madison and Jay 1961, 78). And the reason he was concerned about crowds being "actuated by some common impulse of passion" is because, as he stated in paper 55, "passion never fails to wrest the scepter from reason" (1961, 342).

A perfect example of the fickleness and inflammatory nature of a human pack shows up clearly in Scripture. One can easily see how the hordes welcoming Jesus at the triumphal entry turn on him, at the instigation of the religious elites, within the week, crying out, "Crucify him! Crucify him!" The same thing happens in Acts 14:8–20. There, Paul and Barnabas enter the municipality of Lystra, a town in the south-central region of modern-day Turkey. While announcing the good news of Jesus Christ, they end up healing a man. And "when the crowds saw" what had been done, they break out in a commotion, chanting "The gods have come down to us in the likeness of men!" It took quite a bit of effort for Paul and Barnabas to calm the masses. Yet, in an instant, the crowd is thrown into a fuss and is nearly unrestrained.

Just a few days later, instigators from other regions come flowing into Lystra and quickly change the peoples' minds about Paul and Barnabas. Once more, it's a mob breaking out in a furor, "having persuaded the crowds, they stoned Paul and dragged him out of the city, supposing that he was dead." The crowds had recently declared their awe of, and excitement toward, Paul and Barnabas. And now the residents of the same town are thrown into crowdsourced violence.

This kind of mob mentality surfaces on social media and in our streets, and it follows a simple set of traits. For example, Courtroom Sciences, Inc., provides its clients with consulting help during dramatic events that threaten to turn viral and break into a social media crisis. As they describe it, the psychology of online mobs shares these elements: First, there's a *triggering event*, some incident that causes concern or alarm. Then there's a story that is published and "spins into a narrative that engenders moral outrage." Next comes a lack of faith by those following the story "that justice will prevail." Finally, a "flashpoint is reached. Anonymous, uncredentialed individuals post false information, unfounded opinions, and moralistic posturing—feeding each other's speculations and calling for action in the name of justice and the public good." Then, the article points out a stark reality, "If all four elements are in place, you've reached a point where calls to reason and a measured response are typically met with increased fury" (Murphy and Boesen n.d.).[11]

Whether virtual or in the flesh mobs can be created effortlessly and are deeply dangerous. It is also too easy for one to become caught up in a moral cause fueled by outrage-driven passions and desires that shove out reason, which then transforms a crowd into a hanging party, metaphorically or otherwise.

James, the brother of our Lord, was also concerned about our passions and desires capturing our hearts and actions. "What causes quarrels and what causes fights among you? Is it not this, that your passions are at war within you?

---

11. I would also recommend their article "Why Understanding Mob Mentality Is Key to Creating a Crisis Response Plan" which is on the same website.

You desire and do not have, so you murder. You covet and cannot obtain, so you fight and quarrel" (James 4:1–2a). In the words of Christian counselor Ed Welch, "Desires are not always wrong—we all desire love, respect, adequate money to take care of our families. The problem is that our desires become our rights, or so we believe . . . our desires morph into idols that we live for and that control us" (Welch 2017, 64–65). Passions never fail to wrest the scepter of reason, indeed.

And this is where our topic in this chapter steps in: Suspend judgment. Take a step back from that online outrage or news report, take a breath, don't jump to conclusions, but recall that an accusation is simply an accusation and doesn't equal guilt, and then exhibit the Christian principle that a person is innocent until proven guilty. It all seems fairly straightforward. Very likely these were basic skills in personal relationships we were taught in kindergarten. But, if actions and reactions are any indication, it really is a hard row to hoe for many.

What does it mean to *suspend judgment*? First, it doesn't mean you will never make a decision about the wrongness or rightness of an incident. It does mean you will take a humble position, with its healthy dose of self-doubt, recognizing that you are not *omniscient* (all-knowing) or omnicompetent. Therefore, you accept the reality that you don't likely have all the facts to make an unerring verdict. Second, it is a conscious choice on your part to not allow your passions to wrest the scepter of reason. More specifically, a conscious choice to not allow someone else (reporter, Internet warrior, blogger, "truer-than-others" video) to incite your passions by their demand for immediate action and urgency. You don't have to decide or respond or react right at this moment. As Jonathan Dodson notes, "Outrage culture fosters a rapid, self-righteous response" (Dodson 2020, 137).

Not too many years ago, a particular state in the United States was passing a specific piece of legislation that touched on firearms. As would be expected, a certain group opposed to gun control was up in arms and sought to rouse the citizenry. To do this they put out a news release that seemed to include the wording of the whole law that was being acted on, taking it apart to show how heavy-handed and un-American it was. Someone my family knew started sharing that group's call to action on social media. To my pleasant surprise, my oldest son didn't react immediately but decided to look at the proposed legislation itself and read it for himself. He suspended judgment and took a calm approach. What he found was the pro-gun group had only quoted a portion of the proposed statute and left out the part that actually cancelled their accusations. He then peacefully replied to our friend's social media post and simply pointed out the missing paragraph, quoting it in full, and explained how that paragraph changed the bill into something that wasn't a sinister anti-gun bill. Our friend's post faded off into the virtual mist. Whether you think we should have more gun control or less, the point is that my son suspended judgment; he didn't allow his passions to wrest the scepter of reason and suck him into the swirl of outrage. He then did his own investigation (which took all of ten minutes), saw that the call to action was inaccurate, and kindly pointed out the fallacy without denigrating the friend or the group.

Suspending judgment goes well with Scripture's guidance. Such as, "Do not take to heart all the things that people say, lest you hear your servant cursing you. Your heart knows that many times you yourself have cursed others" (Ecclesiastes 7:21–22). Suspending judgment is part of being as charitable and generous and gracious to others as you want others to be toward you. Maybe an example might be in order.

It still surfaces on social media on occasion, but back in 2018 pictures appeared that were on New York City trash cans, claiming to be authorized by the NYC Sanitation Department. One showed a picture of a white woman carrying a Bible wearing a MAGA hat, the other a white man in a tank top T-shirt with a Confederate flag tattoo and wearing a MAGA hat. The caption at the top of each was *Keep NYC Trash Free.* Someone I knew put the picture out on his Facebook feed. Instead of getting incensed about the picture, jumping to a hasty conclusion, and becoming part of an Internet mob, I decided to suspend judgment and do my own research through different news sources. What came to light was that an artist-activist had created the adhesive signs and attached them to city trash bins. The NYC Sanitation Department quickly issued a statement declaring that they did not authorize these displays, and promptly removed them. The artist-activist has since displayed similar "Facebook ads." Even though the pictures were old news, they were still being shown as though this was happening now. Suspending judgment allowed me to do a little digging around, which took all of ten minutes, and immediately recognize that neither NYC nor their Sanitation Department endorsed such derogatory statements. If I had not suspended judgment, and reined in my passions, I could have easily slipped into outrage, called the NYC Sanitation Department, and demanded that heads roll. It would have made their day miserable, and it would have made me look the fool.

What I'm aiming for, this recognition that we need to learn to suspend judgment, shows up in other settings as the way of getting healthy in relationally sick situations. For example, Megan Hunter and Andrea LaRochelle wrote a workbook for parents going through a divorce with a high-conflict person, *The High-Conflict Co-Parenting Survival Guide.* In one of their short chapters, they point out how high-conflict people set relational fires and want the other spouse to run around in a panic and put them out. Then the authors write, "Learning to hit pause is a response pattern that takes a lot of work to re-write. Not only does your co-parent tell you everything needs to happen ASAP, but new technologies put the pressure on. You may think if you hit pause, you might miss something. So what? You might miss something and some fires might burn longer than if you weren't putting your conflict on pause . . . You might, you just might, learn that's all okay anyway. You don't need to be a living life/managing conflict superhero" (Hunter and LaRochelle 2019, 80–81). I love that last line. *You don't need to be a living life/managing conflict superhero!* And it's the same regarding reports and posts and tweets and podcasts. We don't need to be ramped up to become managing conflict/moral outrage superheroes.

Several years ago, I received an email from a parishioner. It felt like it was full of accusations, and I immediately reacted by writing a reply that was very defensive and driven. Just as I was about to click the send button, I had a moment of pause hit me. I left the email and my hot reply to sit in my draft folder for about three hours. When I had finally calmed myself, cooled down, and collected my thoughts,

I returned and reread the original email that I initially thought was hostile. To my chagrin I found that it was a cry for help, a heartbroken person on the verge of an emotional breakdown. I was deeply ashamed of my misreading and my knee-jerk reaction to ardently defend myself. It likely would have been a hammer blow to a bruised and fragile heart. I deleted my initial reply and wrote one that was empathetic and compassionate. If at first I had suspended judgment, I might not have elevated my heart rate and wasted my time and emotional energies drafting such an inappropriate reply.

The first three concepts of this book go together and undergird what it means to <u>validate before you palpitate; authenticate before you propagate</u>. First, remember that accusation simply means accusation, and does not equal guilt. Take the stance that a person is innocent until proven guilty. Finally, suspend judgment. If a reader gets these first three practices into their normal ingestion of media input, it will put them light-years ahead of many of their compatriots. It will empower them to keep their heads on straight when others are running around with their hair on fire. It will fortify them as they don't allow other people or incidents to take over their passions. James Madison was correct that passions never fail to wrest the scepter from reason.

And these three traits will similarly give us new sensibilities on how to see media, reporters, and reports. Together, these will furnish us with the ability to move beyond outrage.

Before we go any further, though, let's take a break and consider what it means to post with peacemaking on the brain.

Practice for the Week:

- As you run across different types of media sources, keep an eye and ear out for "this is urgent" messages that subtly, or demonstrably, advocate that we simply accept their "facts," become irate, and act now.
- Take some time to scroll through your Instagram notifications or other social media statements with an eye to the underlying message, rather than the content. Is the wording intended to gather a virtual (or literal) mob for a "lynching"—to

shut down someone, shame them, get them fired, hang them out to dry, or other actions? If so, ask yourself, "How is this any different from the angry taxi drivers storming the jail and murdering Willie Earle?"

- When you find a headline or article or "meme" catching your attention and raising your blood pressure, stop and remind yourself you don't know all the facts. You're not omniscient nor omnicompetent. Then take out your notepad and write out details and proofs you will need answered before you give your verdict.

- Take one reported incident or news story or opinion piece that you think is good and strong. Then, (1) become the "devil's advocate" for a moment. Think through what those who disagree might see in that testimony or commentary or incident. Consider what questions they might ask, why, and what evidence they would need to be given to help convince them. (2) Go the other direction and ponder what it would take to make this or that article or opinion piece stronger.

MICHAEL W. PHILLIBER

INTERLUDE: POSTING WITH PEACEMAKING ON THE BRAIN

We've seen it more times than we care to count. Someone puts out their opinion, sometimes stating it as fact, on social media, then within minutes snarky replies show up in the comments. The snarky begins to devolve into the snide, then the spiteful, and finally into an outright extreme virtual cage fight. The saddest part is that maybe some of the combatants claim to be Christians or are people we know. This scene has become so endemic that social media and verbal fistfights have become synonymous. Therefore, Douglas S. Bursch, copastor of Evergreen Foursquare Church in Auburn, Washington, former newspaper columnist and talk radio host, has presented a timely work addressing this exact phenomenon. *Posting Peace: Why Social Media Divides Us and What We Can Do About It* is a 208-page paperback that delves into the way we are online, its consequences, and how to approach our Internet presence with a whole new set of methods. The author's premise is that "social media platforms are structured to separate us from some of the most basic interactions we need to establish strong relationships. The online medium fosters and exaggerates non-reconciling behavior" and it "normalizes and codifies bad behavior" (Bursch 2021, 5). The book is a much-needed work, and worth the time to engage.

Bursch is writing specifically for Christians, since we're expected to magnify the God and Father of our Lord Jesus Christ in all we do. As the apostle Paul states, "So, whether you eat or drink, or whatever you do, do all to the glory of God. Give no offense to Jews or to Greeks or to the church of God" (1 Corinthians 10:31–32). The author takes this position seriously and demonstrates (1) the ways we easily defy the biblical injunction, and (2) the numerous behaviors we can practice that embody this scriptural directive. For example, because of the kind of people we're supposed to be, then sometimes "this requires that we step away from the trending chaos of the online crowd to pray, read God's

Word, and find God's heart. Too often the immediacy of social media keeps us from pausing to consider the perspective of our reconciling Savior. How many conflicts could be handled better if we first took time to find the heart of God before we post, tweet, or hit send?" (126). This volume is full of challenges to our "normal" practices and gives plenty of encouragements to inhabit a new normality.

One of Bursch's principal perspectives is that social media is shaping us, molding our characters, and forming our relational interactions. He states clearly that what "becomes normalized in our social media practices becomes standardized in our marriages, families, and friendships. What we do online and how we do it online have consequences that go far beyond the online world" (28). Readers will face this concept from one end of the book to the other and will also be met by numerous examples of their habitual online traits. The way out of this morass, so we can go further up and further on, is to see ourselves as peacemakers. Thus, for "us to be peacemakers we must intentionally humanize every online interaction" (120). This is not a go-along-to-get-along approach, but a perspective, an aim, an endeavor we should be reaching for, even when we are addressing real injustices and inequities.

The book is stuffed full of material from plenty of sources and studies. Though a reader may periodically come to a different conclusion than the author regarding one of the studies or other, nevertheless, this volume is not simply the writer's opinion. There are enough references and reports to cause one to slow down and take stock. I found the endnotes useful in tracing down a few of the findings that surface throughout this present work.

My only disappointment was the way the book speaks to injustice, and the idea of white privilege. For example, while untangling the messiness of online arguing, the author addresses the reaction of avoidance and disengagement. His remedy is to refute conflict avoidance and extrication from social media skirmishes and to encourage readers to get in there and mix it up, because true "societal transformation comes through challenging the injustices of society and the people who promulgate those injustices" (75). It struck me as an oddity in a book that was all about peacemaking. Truly, there is a place when addressing a wrong might be right, but there are other times where taking the slow, nearly silent approach seems more biblical and beneficial. I'm thinking of our Lord's direction to talk with a person privately first and try to resolve the situation at the lowest level of relational engagement (Matthew 18:15–20). One could, and should, peruse Proverbs and notice how often silence, calmness, and slowness to respond is the epitome of God-fearing wisdom. Bursch develops his position more fully in a later chapter, "When Justice Demands Conflict" (146–161), in which he assumes conflict avoidance comes from white privilege. I had a hard time stomaching that chapter.

Nevertheless, even with that disappointment noted, *Posting Peace* is a work worth its weight in gold! My fellow Christian ministers and leaders must snag a copy, pore over it, and employ many of the author's suggestions. In fact, anyone who finds themselves interacting on social media, and claims to be a Christian, ought to stop publishing online for two weeks and devote that time to reading this work. The consequences for utilizing the concepts in this manuscript will be huge, as we learn to "respond to the instantaneous, polarizing individualism of social media with the thoughtful, self-giving, other-focused reconciling example of Christ" (168). If I could wave a magic wand to get people to purchase and read one book in 2023, other than my own, this would be the volume!

Now, back to our main program.

HANLON'S RAZOR

Accusation Does Not Mean Guilt

Guilty until Proven Innocent?

Suspend Judgment

Hanlon's Razor

Human Reporters

Reasonable Explanations

Media Angle

Over-Reporting

When I think of it now, it makes me chuckle. But when it happened, I cringed, did a "face-palm," and groaned. I had just taken the position of pastor at a small, young church in West Texas. One of the parishioners knew the local paper's religion editor and arranged for me to be interviewed for a "New Pastor in Town" article. The day and time arrived, and up came the excited reporter. She was a member of another conservative church in town and was delighted to find out about me and our congregation. The interview lasted around one hour and was clearly a Christian-friendly conversation. About a week later the article was printed for all to see, and I was aghast. The correspondent had specific interests she wanted to capitalize on and was excited that we agreed. The problem came about because she spent most of the article making those few interests the point of the whole article, which made me, and the congregation, look like a cult that wanted to hole up in a compound in the hinterlands of West Texas. My first thought was, "Wow! And this was someone on our side, someone friendly to us! I wonder what would have happened if she had not been a friend?"

That personal story leads me to mention a tenet I have found immensely helpful at multiple levels. It's known as "Hanlon's razor." This little maxim shows up in mildly different forms, and is attributed to Robert J. Hanlon, an author and professor. The version of the adage I find useful in more situations than I can count is: *Never ascribe to malice that which is adequately explained by incompetence.* It is an explanatory perception and one more tool to help us move beyond outrage.

Once you have this saying in your head, it changes the way you think about what you hear in public, such as when governors make decisions and proclamations. Most of the time, it's not because they have malice in their heart and want to wipe out or shut down one specific group or other. I assume first off, unless I know otherwise, that it's a simple case of incompetence and neglect. And that makes itself clear in time. As you apply Hanlon's razor to more governmental decisions you begin to realize how often they are not really thinking about any one group. Almost always they are about fitting this set of circumstances into a paradigm or standard that a government agency has set up. You come to see that the decisions are more from incompetence than malice when it makes little sense, and you start thinking in your head, "That's weird. They're not making the best of decisions. What's wrong with those people?"

This adage, to never ascribe to malice that which is adequately explained by incompetence, gives us one more question to ask while we're validating our media. Was this reported incident, or that journalist's approach in their article, really a malicious action with malicious intent, or is it more likely a result of incompetence? The young woman who interviewed me was friendly, was on our side, and yet she got things skewed and slanted until it was off base. Malice? No. Incompetence? Most likely.

Here are some genuine headlines, which are quite humorous, that give us a sense of how sloppiness, or incompetence, surfaces in the news.

- "State Population to Double by 2040; Babies to Blame"
- "Federal Agents Raid Gun Shop, Find Weapons"
- "One Armed Man Applauds the Kindness of Strangers"
- "Statistics Show That Teen Pregnancy Drops Off Significantly after Age 25"
- "Homicide Victims Rarely Talk to Police"

Those are amusing and make us laugh. They also emphasize the humanness of reporters, journalists, and editors, and why Hanlon's razor is far more accurate in its assessment than our immediately assuming evil intent. Never ascribe to malice that which is adequately explained by incompetence.

But there are more serious issues when it comes to press and news coverage. These other types of broadcasts and journalistic approaches are common. Keep Hanlon's razor in mind as we delve into them, it will help you stay grounded.

There are sensational or attention-grabbing news reports. For example, this was a real headline, "A NASA Probe May Have Found Signs of Life on Venus 40 Years Ago." The article was penned by Jonathan O'Callaghan and showed up in the 1 October 2020 edition of *Scientific American*. That headline is shocking and makes you stop and do a double take, which is the point. When you read the article, you discover that it's not what we would normally call signs of life but was about some gas that normally comes about when there are microbes present. Yet it's not necessarily a sign of life. In fact, six weeks later *Scientific American* came back with another article that retracted the initial assertion and said (I'm paraphrasing), "Well, the scientists that said all this about signs of life, and such, are now backing off and saying it really is not a sign of life, it's just stuff, you know, that's out there." The initial headline is the sensational attention-grabbing reportage.

But why would news outlets get involved in sensational attention-grabbing headlines and news articles? Clearly, they want to grab your attention, so you'll read the article, or click on the link. Yet why would they want you to do that? It's primarily to increase readership, which translates into making more money. The more people read their articles, the more the statistics become increasingly impressive, which they can then hand to advertising clients and say, "See, this is why you need to advertise with our paper/news outlet." And why is that important? It's important because their journalists are all hungry and the employees need the money. This is really straightforward, and there's nothing malicious in it. This is what we call the free market. All of us capitalists should be saying in our heads, "Yeah, okay, I get it. I have that figured out." Now, it doesn't excuse the misleading nature of such headers, but it's good for us to remember that as we're looking at these captions there are times, though not all the time, when these titles are intended to draw us in so we'll look, and they can then snatch a little bit bigger piece of the advertising money.

The most easily seen sensational attention-grabbing ploy is the online media material that is known as *"clickbait."* Big captions that are meant to stir up our lusts, fears, worries, alarms, cravings for juicy gossip, etc. and get us to stop a bit at their page so that while we're perusing the goodies, they flood us with 101 ads. There are even websites that have manuals and guides to show all the right words to use in the headline to get more people to click on the article. *Clickbait* is just what it sounds like. Dramatic headlining so readers will stop scrolling through news feeds and land on their caption, click on it, and—viola! —they have another "hit" they can show their advertisers. Annoying? Yes. Malicious? Well, not any more malicious than that phone call you recently received to warn you that your car's extended warranty has expired.

There is also a kind of reporting that has been termed as *"yellow journalism."* This is normally where an article, to get the lion's share of readers and promote a specific agenda, presents an explicitly angled view of events, sometimes with outright accusations. The classic example, of course, was the *New York Journal*, owned and run by William Randolph Hearst, Sr., back in the late 19th century. His paper was in a heated contest with Joseph Pulitzer and his *New York World*. The moment came when the USS *Maine* was in Cuba's Havana Harbor to provide protection for American interests in Cuba, as some of the Cuban locals had revolted against Spain. On February 15, 1898, the USS *Maine* was hit by an explosion, and 260 members of the crew were killed. Before any investigation or report on the causes of explosion had been accomplished, on the 17th of February, just two days after the incident, Hearst's publication printed the headline "Destruction of the War Ship *Maine* Was the Work of an Enemy" and offered a $50,000 reward to find the perpetrator "of the *Maine* Outrage!" Hearst went on in an editorial of that edition to accuse Spain of attacking a US warship. Not long after, the short Spanish–American War broke out. Now, the reporting was not the cause of the Spanish–American War, but it had quite a bit to do with it. And, in certain ways, the newspaper ended up helping create the very news events it reported on. Malice? Possibly. Incompetence? Just as likely.

One more set of examples is in order. It has to do with reporters' and readers' assumptions. On the 6th of April in 2021, an eye-catching headline surfaced from STAT News and showed up in my paper. The banner stated, "1 in 3 Covid-19 Patients Are Diagnosed with a Neuropsychiatric Condition in the Next Six Months, Large Study Finds" (Cooney 2021). When I initially read this, I was alarmed. I read it as one out of every three people who have had COVID-19 showed up with neuropsychiatric complications. The word *"patient"* isn't a group-specific class of people to me. Patients could be a broad group of people who have been sick, tested positive, and recovered. It wasn't until I read deep into the article, down around the fifth paragraph, that it slowly dawned on me that the writer was using *patient* to refer to people admitted into the hospital. The writer assumed I knew what she meant by the word *patient.* And I assumed she meant something else. Sometimes reporters' and readers' assumptions are different.

The very next day came a CNBC article based on the STAT News piece, with a slightly different title, "1 in 3 Covid Survivors Suffers Neurological or Mental Disorders, Study Finds" (Ellyatt 2021)[12]. That title changed *"patient"* to *"survivors."* It's not until the third bullet point

12. You can easily find an almost identical title at Reuters that is written with a slightly different focus.

you realize these are "survivors" who had been hospitalized. It seems clear to me that the author of the CNBC version had read the original title from STAT News the way I did, where *patient* was a broader group of people. Instead of either article being misleading, everyone was making assumptions, both reporters and readers, and they didn't initially connect. It took attentive reading, and some deductive reasoning, to get to the correct point of the articles.

One extra piece to add to this picture is this: Depending on the paper, the author of an article might not be the one who comes up with the title. In many cases, a harried and hurried editor throws one onto the news story, and off it goes to the physical or virtual printer. I know as a book author that sometimes the publisher will want to change the title of a book I've written, which might be for the better, or might stir controversy.

This little foray into the various types of articles and reports is to give us an opportunity to see Hanlon's razor: Never ascribe to malice that which is adequately explained by incompetence. Call me naïve, but I have discovered that this perspective is far healthier than assuming the media is out to get us.

I find that the approach of Hanlon's razor goes well with the wisdom of Scripture. For example, "Whoever diligently seeks good seeks favor, but evil comes to him who searches for it" (Proverbs 11:27). To seek out what is good in someone's actions or demeanor lends itself to finding favor with them. But to assume evil intent, and look into others' actions assuming evil intent, means I will, most likely and very easily, find evil intent—even if there is none.

Also Hanlon's razor jives with the caution of Ecclesiastes, "Do not take to heart all the things that people say, lest you hear your servant cursing you. Your heart knows that many times you yourself have cursed others" (Ecclesiastes 7:21–22). If I take every action and word I see and hear to heart, especially what surfaces in all platforms of media, then I will likely have a heart attack. Far better to never ascribe to malice that which is adequately explained by incompetence.

Hanlon's razor also goes well with our Lord's statement in Luke 6:36–38, and how we're to treat others just as charitably and generously and graciously as we want them to treat us. When I have done things that disturbed people, or said things that got them incensed, I would far rather they see most of my foibles as arising from my incompetence rather than malice, because most of my faults are due to my own personal ineptitudes.

Therefore, to <u>validate before we palpitate and authenticate before we propagate</u> requires that we do a few things. First, we remind ourselves that accusation does not equal guilt. Then, we take the position of innocent until proven guilty. Next, we suspend judgment. And subsequently, we don't immediately ascribe to malice that which is adequately explained by incompetence.

This leads us to the next segment that I have already begun hinting at here. Reporters are human.

Practice for the Week:

- Search your local news sources for article titles that seem to say one thing, but, after reading the article, you find it changes the meaning of the headline.

- Run through your news feeds and try to distinguish from the titles between news sources and clickbait.

- When a friend shares an article or news report, whatever the source, slowly read through every word of each paragraph. Write down how each piece repeats what was previously written, and how each section adds a new detail that changes a bit of the story. Then, review the article deciding on which parts are assertion and which are reports of factual details.

- Find an article about the decision of a local or state governmental official. As you read it think, "Never ascribe to malice that which is adequately explained by incompetence." Now, describe how Hanlon's razor changes the way you evaluate that particular account.

MICHAEL W. PHILLIBER

HUMAN REPORTERS

Accusation Does Not Mean Guilt
Guilty until Proven Innocent?
Suspend Judgment
Hanlon's Razor
Human Reporters
Reasonable Explanations
Media Angle
Over-Reporting

If you didn't know it, reporters are human. At least, human reporters are human. There is an artificial intelligence (AI) program out there that can accomplish AI-generated essays and articles (GPT-3). For the most part reporters are human. This means that, well, they're human with all of the limitations of knowledge, emotion, finitude, and inexperience.

When Nicole Charky-Chami started her journalism career after college, she worked at the *Los Angeles Times* and as an overnight breaking news reporter for *City News Service*, which is Southern California's newswire. This means that she pulled "all-nighters" at the Los Angeles Police Department (LAPD) listening to scanners, scouring the Internet and other sources for tips, etc.

In 2011, Bryan Stow, a Giants fan, was badly beaten at Dodger Stadium in the parking lot. He was beaten into a coma, suffering brain injuries. On the day after the attack there was another game at Dodger Stadium, where security was increased because of concern for safety and more potential troubles. The editor asked Charky-Chami to call the LAPD Northeast Station to see if there had been any arrests. The watch commander told her there had been 100 arrests. If she had taken a moment to clarify, she would have realized it was 100 citations, not arrests. But she raced off a report with misinformation, which quickly got picked up by newswire subscribers, TV stations, newspapers, and radio news broadcasters. Once the mistake was found, they all had to run corrections (Charky-Chami 2019).

To have reported 100 arrests would make it seem that a riot, brawl, or large demonstration had broken out, and might be an indication of worse things happening. But 100 citations being issued is closer to drunken displays, disturbing the peace, and traffic violations. Not double-checking the facts in this situation momentarily spread unintentional misinformation and embarrassed the reporter and many news sources. Reporters are human.

When we recognize that reporters are human, it should alter how we receive the news. Just as reporters need to double-check and triple-check their facts, we also need to make double sure that we have the facts. We must <u>validate before we palpitate and authenticate before we propagate</u>.

Biases

Since reporters are human, this obviously means they have their own biases. A correspondent's own enthusiasm will govern what is narrated and what is left out of the narration. If they're really animated about a topic, it clearly comes out. Think about the woman who interviewed me for a "New Pastor in Town" article, how she was on our side, and yet her particular bias governed what she wrote. It makes logical sense.

We're all biased in this way or that. I don't like coconut or okra. If I were a reporter, I might not be so attentive or enthused about covering okra crop failures. But asparagus! Now we're talking. And I would most likely do a seriously investigative piece on asparagus crop failures, or production. It all sounds silly, and I mean it that way. But it's even sillier when recipients of the news expect their broadcasters or writers to be 100% right, and to assume that any misinformation is because of malice. Hanlon's razor should be a help here. Never ascribe to malice that which is adequately explained by incompetence. Biases are part of our own daily inefficiencies. Reporters are human.

Social Media Sources

Another way that reporters' humanness shows up is in what they consider as a viable news source. One of those places that Nicole Charky-Chami looked for leads and information was social media. In fact, Dr. Alecia Swasy, a Reynolds Journalism Institute scholar, presented a report to the institute and their AP research forum, "Setting or Chasing the Agenda: Who Controls the News?" In that paper, she records a study that was done by two researchers who did a content analysis of about 2,000 articles over a six-year period from the *New York Times* and the *Washington Post*, and they found that the newspapers used blogs as credible sources. She goes on to write, "Between 30 to 40 percent of the *Times* and *Post* articles cited blogs as sources" (Swasy n.d.).

Swasy further observes,

> "Twitter has become a player in setting the national agenda for coverage of politics. CNN journalist Peter Hamby (2013) interviewed more than 70 journalists and political strategists who worked on the 2012 presidential campaigns. The case study focused on Republican Nominee Mitt Romney's campaign. Hamby concluded that the instantaneous nature of social media now means any gaffe or stumble now becomes the story, sometimes within minutes. Hamby asserts that Twitter is

> now the central news source for the Washington-based political press corps."

I asked several people how many of them read and accept blogs, Twitter tweets, Facebook posts, etc. as credible sources. The numbers are decreasing, but often a significant portion of those I ask think this is the case. We're human. Reporters are human. Part of the point to take away from this, which Swasy makes in her paper, is that "the media coverage is setting the nation's public agenda." But unlike earlier decades, such as the 1968 elections, "this time, the agenda is being shaped by citizens, too." That means our posts, our tweets, our blogs, etc., are setting the direction of a significant portion of the news. Let that sink in for a moment before you move on.

Inaccuracies

Back in September 2005, Scott R. Maier wrote a paper for the *Journalism & Mass Communication Quarterly*. The article was titled "Accuracy Matters: Cross-Market Assessment of Newspaper Error and Credibility" (Maier 2005).

In that piece he noted that a "survey of 4,800 news sources cited in fourteen newspapers provides a cross-market assessment of newspaper accuracy and the effect of errors on newspaper credibility. Sources found errors in 61% of local news and feature stories, an inaccuracy rate among the highest reported in nearly seventy years of accuracy research." He goes on to observe how the study showed that "neither stature of the paper nor market size appears to be closely associated with accuracy or credibility as perceived by sources."

Undoubtedly, these studies and articles are not attempting to excuse poor reporting. In fact, in all of the sources I've read, the constant theme is "We journalists can do better. So, let's do better." Yet we, the readers and listeners of the news, know that reporters are human. Which means, we should know that errors will arise. Therefore, though there may be moments when malicious misinformation happens, more times than not, it's the humanity of the reporter we should accept. Because reporters are human, it's far better we suspend judgment, and not immediately ascribe to malice that which is adequately explained by incompetence.

Inexperience

I find it interesting that most consumers of the news fail to recognize a simple aspect of the reporter's humanity. Because journalists are genuine people, they are not omnicompetent. Therefore, they have a limited frame of experience from which they write. Most correspondents have a bachelor's degree in journalism, and possibly an internship. Hopefully, the internship included a wise coach. But, at twenty-two or twenty-three years of age, armed with a degree and a small package of experiences, and biases, they launch into the world to report—often times, on events or subjects beyond their experience or knowledge.

I know a man who used to work for the Federal Aviation Administration (FAA). For over thirty years, he was tasked with investigating airplane accidents. Once the inquiry was completed, and the findings presented to the proper authorities, he would then write up press releases. And he said to me, with frustration, that in that thirty-plus-year tenure of handing the media these press releases, the reporters still got details and facts wrong. And then he stated, "They have no experience in aviation, and have no idea what they were writing about." Reporters are human.[13]

---

13. We will return to my FAA friend in the concluding chapter.

Inexperience plays out, for example, when correspondents are writing about most things Christian. If the numbers are correct, many journalists are not Christian, or no longer consider themselves as Christian. Imagine if a reporter grew up in a Muslim family and was sent out to report on a burglary at a church, where the bandits took off with a Communion chalice and consecrated bread. Now, imagine how that writer's ignorance of Christianity will look in their article when they hear talk about the Eucharist, and some chatter about the body and blood of Jesus. Is it a surprise that this correspondent might actually get things wrong, maybe even horribly wrong? If the editor also has limited knowledge of Christianity, then is it any wonder that some strange details might show up in the article? Instead of assuming malice, remember reporters are human, and so the first place to go is to recognize the likelihood of their incompetence due to inexperience.

Haste

One last area to take note of is haste. I mentioned in a previous chapter that the pressure is on, and reporters are rushed to put out their stories with a sense of urgency. The paper or establishment wants to be the first one to break the news so that they will get the lion's share of readers/listeners and can show their clients why advertising with their agency is a good investment. Add to this the speed of the Internet and worldwide news, and the burden is less on investigation and more on "Get it out there!" The rush to the presses, then, sets up a breeding ground for potential inaccuracies and other problems. Why? Because reporters are human. How many mistakes have you made when rushing to get a project done and you had a hard deadline? Therefore, no need to immediately jump to the conclusion that a misreported event was due to malice. Haste can lead to incompetence.

Turning the Gaze

At this point it is useful to turn to Christian media sources and apply the same standards. What I mean is, Christian correspondents are also human. Therefore, we need to be sensible and recognize that they too are biased. They too, most likely, use social media as a resource. They too channel inaccuracies in their reports. They too report, most often, from a lack of experience. And they too are being pressured to rush their findings to the presses. Christian media reports, news pieces, broadcasts, etc. should be vetted with the exact same level of scrutiny that we use on other media. Christian news voices should also be treated with the same assumption that, more often than not, malice is not likely the cause of a misreport, but incompetence.

An easy illustration might be when Christian news sources report on the persecution of Christians in other countries. It can all sound very disconcerting and get people wound up tight. A news reader (and reporter, for that matter) needs to begin further back. The incident happens where one tribe or a government moves into a region and begins to destroy a Christian tribe. Before it immediately becomes "persecution" news, a few questions should be asked and answered. Have these two tribes been at odds before? Does this conflict go back, per chance, to pre-Christian days? Is this simply another incident where one clan, who happen to be of a different faith, is pouring out vengeance for something that happened in a previous generation? Are they seeking vengeance at the expense of a clan that just happens to be Christian? If it's a government assault on a specific tribe, one needs to ask, "Is that national government a certain empowered tribe that has been at odds with this Christian tribe, maybe even back to their pre-Christian days?" If Ethiopia and Rwanda are examples where a Christian tribe rises up against a Christian tribe, then, news readers (and reporters) need to move beyond their narrow frame of reference and limited experience, do a little research, and answer some of these basic questions before they broadcast persecution reports.

To conclude, none of these human tendencies excuse journalists or give them license to be sloppy and never tighten up their reporting. But stating the reality of these trends helps us to slow down, recognize what is most likely the case, validate our news reports, not villainize our reporters unnecessarily, and move beyond outrage.

Before we go any further, there's a pause just a page ahead, where we will take a moment to hear about "Grandstanding."

Practice for the Week:

- Take an article or newscast from your favorite news source. List out what details they announce. Now, go to another news source, maybe one you don't like. See how they report on that event and write down the details that stick out to you. What are the differences? What are the similarities? Are there any new details? What were their sources of information?

- Now, find a third news source recording this event, one that comes from a foreign country. Or one that is publicly funded. See how they report the incident. Jot down the differences, similarities, and any new details.

- As you have time this week, follow this approach on three or four other events. Do you notice any trends of how each source "reports" the particulars? Did you find any of these broadcasts or newspapers misreporting information? Where did you look to get the accurate data? Was there anything else you observed that is noteworthy?

- How much did the humanity of the journalist play into each report?

INTERLUDE: GRANDSTANDING

It's melting the Internet and burning up several news outlets. It makes informed dialogue among people nearly impossible, cracking up the sense of, and desire for, the common good. It looks and feels like chest-thumping and cock-strutting. It's turning up with greater intensity in the White House, the publishing house, and at the alehouse. Not long ago, a well-documented 248-page hardback arrived on the scene diagnosing this "more-heat-than-light" predicament: *Grandstanding: The Use and Abuse of Moral Talk.* The authors, Justin Tosi, Assistant Professor of Philosophy at Texas Tech University, and Brandon Warmke, Assistant Professor of Philosophy at Bowling Green State University, want to foster moral talk, but find huge obstacles. "People need to be able to talk about justice, freedom, equality, and the right thing to do. But we need to do so in ways that do good, and not just make ourselves look good. Grandstanders are too concerned with the latter" (Tosi and Warmke 2020, ix). It's an easy-to-read volume, accessible to older students, professors, pastors, and folks from almost any walk of life.

Grandstanding has a simple order to it. After the bird's-eye view in the preface, the authors then draw out seven chapters that expose what grandstanding is, how it looks and sounds on social media all the way to politics. The final chapter is a "What do we do with this knowledge?" chapter and goes where readers may not fully expect. Each section is chock-full of true-to-life, documented illustrations, and careful analysis of every case. And the endnotes are splashing over with references and documentation. It may be a smallish book, but it carries a weighty credibility.

Tosi and Warmke promote the value and significance of moral talk. From one end of the volume to the other, they stand up for it (6). The problem, as they see it, is that grandstanding persistently shuts down moral conversation. "Unfortunately, many people use moral talk irresponsibly. They use it to humiliate, intimidate, and threaten people they dislike, impress their friends, feel better about themselves, and make people less suspicious about their own misconduct . . . For these people, moral talk is magic . . .

magically transforms your nasty, abusive, self-ish behavior into something heroic and praise-worthy" (5). Taking this approach, then, under-mines our efforts at moral improvement (6, 10). Grandstanding also turns public discourse into a war of moral one-upmanship (10).

Why do people grandstand? Tosi and Warmke give several motives (14–23). There is recognition desire, where we want others to think we're morally impressive and respect-able. There is also the urge to dominate others. This is the move one makes to take others down a notch or three with a "Shut up and submit to my view of the world or I'll shame and embar-rass you! I'm the morally good one here" (17)! Another intention is the need to express our-selves in ways "to get people to believe that" we "are morally special" (18). The authors further tackle the various techniques people use, such as implication, indirect language, humblebrag-ging, and moral self-enhancement, to name a few.

The grandstanding Tosi and Warmke are talking about can be easily described by the windshield analogy. Recently, my youngest son, a college graduate, began to wax eloquent—like his dad has been known to do. We were sitting around the dinner table, both adult sons, my wife and I, and we were talking about people's angry, polemical actions on social media. My youngest son jumped up and said, "Dad, this is like the windshield." I smartly replied, "Huh?" "Think along with me, dad," he went on. "We know lots of wonderful people, gracious, kind, friendly, but some of them turn into vicious people when they get into their cars and get behind their windshield. That windshield separates them from real flesh-and-blood people, and because they don't have to interact with other people that they can see face-to-face, they become nasty, judgmental, throwing out loud, demeaning remarks at the other drivers." I thought, "What a brilliant son I have sired!" That's very much how grandstanding works.

One of the humorous findings the authors mention is how people normally think they are more moral than they really are—the illusion of moral superiority (25)—and they present studies that back this up. I appreciated how they clearly show that grandstanding is neither a Republican nor Democrat issue but crosses the political/social spectrum. The downside is that centrists (where most people are) end up shutting themselves out of moral talk because of the grandstanding. In interesting ways, grandstanding hampers and halters freedom of speech (35). Tosi and Warmke bring out several other diagnostic tools, which make this an extremely helpful guide.

This idea of presenting one's moral superiority reminds me of a time back in the early 1980s when I was the bivocational minister of a little church. I was trying to reach people in our community and landed on the idea of doing a Saturday evening religious call-in radio show. I was telling this to another minister who had done a similar broadcast before. I've never forgotten his response to me. He said, "Mike, if you're going to do a religious call-in show, you can never waffle. You have to be certain that you're right, even when you have doubts. You must exude confidence in your position all the time, the moral superiority of your position for every show. If you don't, you'll lose your listeners." I was being coached to grandstand before grandstanding was an item. To tout my moral superiority, even when I had doubts.

According to the authors, grandstanding has been with us all along, but now, with the

ease with which the masses can air their prej-
udices, politics, plots, and plans, it is harder to
avoid seeing grandstanding than ever before
(xi). They are careful not to lay the fault on social media as the main culprit, though many of
their characterizations explode onto every virtual platform one visits.

As a reader dives into the book, it will become clear that the authors are undressing
motivations, and that is a tricky place to be.
Tosi and Warmke recognize this and give
many hearty cautions and healthy counsels.
Ultimately, the book is primarily for the reader
to evaluate themself if they dare. As the authors say early on, this "book is about looking
at ourselves squarely and honestly and asking
whether we are *doing* good with our moral talk,
or just trying to *look* good" (10). That is where
they return in their final chapter, "What to
Do About Grandstanding?" If a reader has any
self-awareness as they read, there will be lots
of internal reflection. As my grandmother used
to say, "Boy, when you point that finger at others, just remember, there are three more pointing right back at you!" I was tempted, page after
page, to wish so-and-so would read this book,

and then found myself hanging my head as I recognized that I have done these very things.

Grandstanding will kick one in the seat of the breeches, but not self-righteously or sanctimoniously. The authors see their own faults and write from that place. This book is perfect for individual readers, book clubs, Adult Christian Education classes, seminary and Bible college classes, and church leadership boards. It is a must, especially if you are engaged on social media or are a public figure. I highly recommend the book.

Back to our regularly scheduled program.

MICHAEL W. PHILLIBER

REASONABLE EXPLANATIONS

Accusation Does Not Mean Guilt
Guilty until Proven Innocent?
Suspend Judgment
Hanlon's Razor
Human Reporters
Reasonable Explanations
Media Angle
Over-Reporting

It was an atrocious situation, and one that can still get blood boiling. But I think it's a fitting introduction to this chapter. It happened on 20 April 2021, a little over a year after Ahmaud Arbery was killed in Georgia, and slightly less than a year after George Floyd was killed while in police custody. Ma'Khia Bryant was residing in a foster home. On this day, an argument broke out between Ma'Khia and others, which heated up and began to spiral out of control. At least one knife was pulled out, and maybe two. As things began to disintegrate, at 4:32 p.m., 911 was called and told that someone was trying to stab somebody. The police arrived at 4:45 p.m. and found Ma'Khia and others fighting, with Ma'Khia wielding a knife. Ma'Khia lunged at one of the girls and shouted that she was going to stab her. The officer fired four shots, and Ma'Khia collapsed and didn't respond to first aid.

More details have since surfaced, from cameras that were recording from different angles, and a fuller story is now known. But in the early hours after the shooting misinformation exploded. Social media posts ran rampant, claiming that the police shot an unarmed black woman. Another post claimed that Bryant herself called the police and approached the officers to explain her situation, and that's when she was shot. Over time, the misinformation was proven wrong, but not before it fueled outrage that turned into protests from locals and university students, spreading from Ohio to Denver, and Florida to California.

The aftermath of this incident shows how potent our reactions are to visual provocations, half-truths, and fabrications. The repercussions also demonstrate how easily convinced people can be to believe the worst and act on that assumption. The most disappointing is when Christians react and immediately suppose what they've "seen" is true, or when believers are quick to level accusations and condemnations based on unverified videos or unsubstantiated charges.

The point of this chapter is that before we react to any news report, or any purportedly true account spread through social media, Christians should take a moment to reflect and consider if there might be other reasonable explanations. The motive for asking if there are other sensible explanations has much to do with God's directions in Scripture.

"You shall not spread a false report. You shall not join hands with a wicked man to be a malicious witness. You shall not fall in with the many to do evil, nor shall you bear witness in a lawsuit, siding with the many, so as to pervert justice, nor shall you be partial to a poor man in his lawsuit" (Exodus 23:1–3). First, notice that spreading a false report goes along with joining hands with a malicious witness.

Next, spreading a false report swims in the same stream with the crowd who are surging forward to do evil or to pervert justice. Lastly, to take a false report, even if you don't know it's false, and to share it or disseminate it, does one of two things (or both). At the least, it mars our credibility. It can give us Christians, who believe the gospel accounts and are supposed to be promoting the truth, a reputation for being gullible or easily deceived, which means that others will have cause to doubt anything we may say. At the worst, it makes us accessories to spreading a false report, accomplices of the slanderous.

Again, to go back to a passage we've looked at before, "The one who states his case first seems right, until the other comes and examines him" (Proverbs 18:17). Matthew Henry, in an online version of his commentary, long ago noted the different aspects of this verse:

> "This shows that one tale is good till another is told. 1. He that speaks first will be sure to tell a straight story, and relate that only which makes for him, and

put the best colour he can upon it, so that his cause shall appear good, whether it really be so or no. 2. The plaintiff having done his evidence, it is fit that the defendant should be heard, should have leave to confront the witnesses and cross-examine them, and show the falsehood and fallacy of what has been alleged, which perhaps may make the matter appear quite otherwise than it did. We must therefore remember that we have two ears, to hear both sides before we give judgment" (Henry [1706] 2022).

Part of biblical stability and sensibility looks for, listens for, and contemplates the possibility of other reasonable answers.

In fact, even thinkers like Jordan Peterson see the value of this attitude. In one of his books he states, "Beware of single cause interpretations—and beware the people who purvey them" (J. Peterson 2018, 311). He was referring, primarily, to those who think everything is a power issue. But I have found this warning a wise perception when defining many things from history to marital difficulties. Single cause interpretations, and those who sell them, are most often wrong. And worse, they foster our jumping to unfounded conclusions that evoke unfounded actions. Instead, we would be better served by thinking through the possibility that there are other reasonable explanations than the one "single cause" interpretation we're being given through our media sources, especially those media sources that are not under any accountability. At least journalists employed by newswires and papers often have to face their editors' scrutiny, even if it's faulty at times. Ask yourself, are there other possible explanations than this single cause interpretation?

Caveat Emptor

When it comes to ingesting the news, viewing video reports, and examining journalistic reports, there is an old Latin adage that is worth applying to our media, whatever the type: *Caveat emptor*. It simply means, "Buyer beware." The saying is meant to remind purchasers of products that they have an obligation to inspect merchandise they are acquiring with some thoroughness.

The same applies to our media sources. Before we buy into a narrative, accept an article's account, embrace a "truer than everybody else" news piece, we should employ *caveat emptor*, buyer beware. Look for other reasonable explanations that might lead you to different conclusions, or fuller descriptions. Look at media angle, notice how narrow a picture is, query the position of the photographer, evaluate the announcer's "take" on the situation compared to other possibilities, look for other viewpoints to the story, and so forth. *Caveat emptor*.

Justice Takes Time

Lastly, I was reading a book on human trafficking and sex trafficking recently. The three authors do a nice job explaining ways we Christians can be part of helping to prevent human trafficking, and more. While they were describing what it takes to prosecute a case against traffickers, they caution Christians to not get caught up in the "flash" of the moment. As they observe,

> "Understanding the problem, assessing community and individual resources, building

relationships with community and government agencies, investigating and building cases, and undertaking the restorative work of healing for survivors take time. They take longer than emotions last, as important as those are in getting us started and reminding us why we do this." Then they go on to state that justice "takes time. And this is justice work. We do not always get to see the fullness of justice work . . ." (Moore, Morgan and Yim 2022, 126–127).

Justice and restoration take longer than emotions last! These observations are worth far more than the gold at Fort Knox. They supplement our theme regarding other possible, reasonable explanations. First, our emotions fuel immediate action. Maybe the incident, and how it is reported, induces our emotional response, inciting us to emotion-fueled action. This obligates us to take a step back and start asking questions to become better informed to make better decisions, which "take longer than emotions last."

Second, justice takes time. Real, genuine justice is slow because our court system grows out of a biblically informed jurisprudence, such as "innocent until proven guilty." Justice takes longer than our emotions last. Justice requires examining other possible explanations. Justice entails looking at evidence, hearing testimony of more than one witness, examining the credibility of witnesses, and working through as many details as is reasonable to come to a just decision. If I were accused of some crime, I would want these slow, judicious procedures for myself. Therefore, an alt news source or legacy news report may want me to be the judge, jury, and executioner now, but justice, real, genuine justice, takes time, and will often take longer than emotions last. Knowing this might actually help us to answer the question we need to ask, "Are there other reasonable explanations?"

Before we take on the next trait, it is important we slow down a moment and consider a word about charitable writing.

Practice for the Week:

- Take an article or social media post
  that has caught your attention, one
  that makes a claim or assertion about
  an incident. On a piece of paper draw a
  line down the center. On the left write
  Article Explanation and on the right
  Other Possible Explanations. Jot down
  under "Article Explanation" the possible
  conclusion the writer wants you to take.
  Note some of the salient facts and details they mention. Then under "Other
  Possible Explanations" list other reasonable (the key word: *reasonable*) analyses
  and evaluations. This may require you to
  do some research on place, time of day at
  that location, the weather that day, and
  so forth. You may even need to review
  other articles covering the same event
  and see if they bring to light information
  missing in your initial account.
- Ask yourself if the conclusion a post or
  blog or podcast or article wants you to
  make is a "single cause interpretation."
  Are there other aspects to the situation

that have been left out, by accident or otherwise, and could the explanation of the affair actually be messier than is being stated?

- Recall Scripture's caution: "The one who states his case first seems right, until the other comes and examines him" (Proverbs 18:17). Cross-examine the post or article. In the words of Matthew Henry noted above, "We must therefore remember that we have two ears, to hear both sides before we give judgment." We also have two eyes to watch out and see if there's more to the story.

- If you have time, take the same steps in the three bullet points above on three other posts or articles. Record your observations.

INTERLUDE: WRITING CHARITABLY

I'm a writer. I have published three books, and this is my fourth. I also write blog posts that include articles, book reviews, and prayers. I pen a weekly letter to my congregation. I type out emails and replies, and I toil over full sermon manuscripts for two sermons a week. I'm a writer. Therefore, my interest was grabbed when I saw *Charitable Writing: Cultivating Virtue through Our Words* arrive on the scene. This 248-page softback was compiled by Richard Hughes Gibson and James Edward Beitler III, both of whom are Associate Professors of English at Wheaton College. It is written primarily with college composition and writing courses in mind—it even has a nice piece in the appendix for teaching the contents of the book. But it is genuinely useful for all writers outside of academia, such as those putting together business proposals, research articles, blogs, sermon manuscripts, pastoral letters, books, essays, or whatever. And the gentle approach the authors take makes this material easily accessible for writers in their teens on out to centenarians.

With a foreword written by Anne Ruggles Gere, and an afterword by Alan Jacobs, the book artfully takes essayists through the principles of writing charitably. Though the book is a writing guide, it's not about comma placements, which voice to use, ways to bring about a concluding statement, paragraph length, run-on sentences, and the like. Instead, it is concerned with "how we *conceive* of and, in turn, *practice* writing" while making an argument "that our spiritual commitments can and should provide bearings for our academic and professional work" (Gibson and Beitler 2020, 1). For the authors, this means that "writing is inescapably bound up with spiritual formation" (9). I found this aim of writing hugely helpful. And especially as Gibson and Beitler point toward one overarching virtue for writing, which is charity founded on humility. In fact, *charitable writing* "is writing that seeks to fulfill the Lord's 'double commandment' to love God and our neighbor" (11). That is the whole book in a nutshell. Each chapter circles back round to this point, page after page, subject after subject, discussion after discussion!

Charitable Writing includes delving deeply into what charity is, as well as humble listening, rightly ordered arguing, "slow writing," and positioning one's composition as a work of learning. It is also about seeing our writing as a work of prayer (165). The authors use "meditations" on sacred art works replicated in the chapters as a way of furthering most subjects and moving the conversation from place to place. The "picturesque" approach didn't resonate with me so much, maybe because I'm an artistic troglodyte, but it did keep things progressing at a good pace.

I found almost every subject rich and rewarding. The discussions that were primarily geared toward academia whizzed past me, but even some of those thoughts were useful. Of all the themes that benefited me, here are two. First, the idea that writing is spiritual formation; it is fostering virtue. And the virtue that we want cultivated most is charity—love of God and neighbor. Coupled with charity comes humility and the importance of writing with humility. I loved their thought, echoing James 4:8a, that states, draw "near to God, charitable writer, and he will draw near to you" (167). Following Augustine, the approach of turning our works into acts of learning and moments of prayer was beautiful.

The other topic I found valuable, even more so in our present outrage culture, was how to develop rightly ordered arguments. Gibson and Beitler lay out the importance of our debate metaphors, which usually circle around war, and give numerous examples of alternative ones that can bring the temperature of an argument down from the charred to a golden, tasty crust (my attempt at another metaphor, yes?). Once the authors show the importance of changing our metaphors, they then give hefty reasons to argue charitably, mapping out ways to accomplish this feat. One aspect is to create the steel man argument. The steel man argument goes like this: Instead of mischaracterizing an opponent's position, we put their case in the best light, clearheadedly restating our interlocutor's view before we give our own response. We listen to hear, rather than listen to respond. Further, using a feast as the backdrop, we write in a way that clearly shows that we are a gracious host at the table, but also a good guest. This whole topic covers three chapters (105–136) and was corrective, perceptive, and indispensable. It made me reflect on how often my thesis adviser had to tone me down while I was working on my doctorate. He would often correct my jargon and reasoning, stating the importance of drawing readers into the discussion instead of throwing them out on their ear. This meant I had to return, rethink, and rewrite for hours. Honestly, being a charitable writer is not for sissies!

Charitable Writing is just too good to let pass by. Are you a blog writer? Get the book. Social Media mogul? Get the book. Researcher or journalist? Get the book. Sermon manuscript author? Get the book. Taking a college class on composition? Get the book. Whoever else I may have missed, just get the book, pore over it, pray, and pen away! As you can tell, I'm sold on it and highly recommend the work to you.

Now, we turn to media angle.

MICHAEL W. PHILLIBER

MEDIA ANGLE

Accusation Does Not Mean Guilt
Guilty until Proven Innocent?
Suspend Judgment
Hanlon's Razor
Human Reporters
Reasonable Explanations
Media Angle
Over-Reporting

There is a drive going on out there, for lack of a better word. It's a group of folks who call themselves First Amendment and Second Amendment auditors. They show up in a town, set up a situation (acting stoned, hiding in the bushes of a city hall or county jail, etc.) and wait until law enforcement is called. Then, when an officer shows up, they begin to act suspicious, keeping their hands behind their back at belt level, barely responding to directions by police officers. Sometimes they will suddenly invade an officer's personal space, and so forth. Usually, unknown to law enforcement, the whole scene is being recorded on video across the street or nearby. If there is an arrest or altercation of any kind, the scene immediately goes out on social media with the intent of giving a sheriff's department or police division a black eye. Normally it's not the whole video that goes out, just a focused scene that may even have a narrator's voice or caption telling you what you're supposed to see happening.

This transpired in Oklahoma City within the last two years. It was the 29th of April in 2021. There was an incident in front of the county jail, and it followed the pattern I mentioned above. The only portion of the video that went out online was when the police officer pushed the suspect to the ground. The narrator described the suspect as giving up when the policeman shoved him. The video immediately hit the social media outlets, and the shouts for "Defund the police!" and "That's proof of cops being abusive" exploded on the Internet.

Within the hour, the Oklahoma City Police Department put out the whole twenty-minute video from the officer's bodycam that started when he exited his squad car until the suspect was handcuffed and placed in the backseat and questioned. It told a completely different story. The officer spent a ton of time trying to get the suspect to take his hand out from behind his back, attempting to communicate to a barely responsive person who acted erratic, who would then walk up close to the officer—within striking distance. It was only after one of those moments when the unpredictable, unresponsive person walked into the police officer's personal space that the officer shoved him back and the man fell. The officer even told him, "Go away, back off, back up!" Both videos showed two totally different stories, but it was the same episode. That evening one of the local television newscasts aired the event from both videos as they reported on the incident. Then the announcer pointed out who the suspect in the video was, Floyd Wallace, and that Wallace was a First Amendment auditor who has been arrested in several other towns and cities for similar actions and having the incidents video recorded.

What was disturbing to me was how easy it was to incite virtual mobs with a short video, one that only broadcasts what the narrator wanted everyone to see and respond to. Once viewers got the bigger picture, the story changed and the hostile responses fizzled. Whether one thinks the officer was right or wrong in the way he acted toward this person, or that First Amendment auditing is a noble action, this was a lesson in how media angle affects viewers' conclusions.

If we keep media angle in mind when watching purported "firsthand videos" of incidents—usually recorded on cellphones that have a very narrow and limited recording range—or when viewing regular newscasts, it will aid us in suspending judgment and compel us to take the time to certify the legitimacy of an incident before we react and respond. Sometimes the firsthand video accounts get it right. At other times, it's only the viewpoint the recorder wants you to see, leaving out details and visual cues that tell a different story. Therefore, to get media angle down correctly, we need to think about personal perception and visual angle.

Personal Perception
In normal situations, sometimes we mis-see or mishear events ourselves. I mentioned in a

previous chapter how my father misheard me, and after disciplining me for what he thought he heard, he corrected himself and apologized. But our perceptions can also be off because of what is called *inattentional blindness.*

The best example of inattentional blindness, or *selective attention,* is a video by Daniel S. Simons called "The Monkey Business Illusion" (Simons 2010). The video has two teams of three people. One team is wearing white, the other is wearing black. Behind them is a red theater curtain. There are two large balls that participants will bounce and pass to each other as they move around in a circle and move between each other. The announcer tells you to count how many times the ball is passed from player to player.

As you, the viewer, are counting the passes, three extra events happen that almost no viewer sees. First, one of the players in a black shirt moves out of the camera view. Then a person in a gorilla suit comes into the scene and stands in the middle for a few seconds, beats his breasts, and walks off. The black-shirted player that went off stage then returns, entering the circle's flow, passing the ball. The last event is that the theater curtain in the background changes colors from red to gold.

The announcer then debriefs those who watched the video. After he tells how many times the ball was passed, he then asks, "Did you see the gorilla?" The majority of audiences never saw the gorilla and are surprised that they missed something so obvious. Once the presenter shows when the gorilla came on and went off, he then asks, "Did anyone see the curtain change colors?" Even the most alert watchers are shocked by having missed that detail. There are other videos using different scenarios that show the same tendency we have in our personal perceptions. We can become so focused in one area we're blind to others.

Inattentional blindness is a part of our human finitude. This means that even a news correspondent is also impacted by inattentional blindness. They too can be caught up in tunnel vision and see only one item while other details are around. This further suggests that reporters can mis-see, mishear, and totally miss additional features. Thus, they can unintentionally misreport, or make mistakes, in their accounts.

Beyond this, there is also an induced inattentional blindness. For example, when the narrator of the First Amendment auditor video tells viewers what we're supposed to be seeing while there's more to the story. It is therefore wise for consumers of the news, when reading a story, or watching video accounts, or newscasts, before they get too emotionally wrapped up or riled by the incident, to ask themselves, "Are there other reasonable explanations for what happened? Are there more facts I need to know about and take into consideration? Is this video only showing part of the story?"

Accusation, even photographic or videoed accusation, does not equal guilt. Suspend judgment, assuming parties are innocent until proven guilty. If, for no other reason, because our own—or the reporter's—personal perceptions can be off or blinded.

There's also the problem of visual angle.

Visual Angle

Not only can personal perception cause us, and journalists, to miss important specifics that might change the explanation of an incident, so can media angle. What I'm referring to here has much to do with visual media, but it also includes the narration that often goes with the graphics. Cameras, cellphone pictures and videos, etc. are very limited in what they can record. Based on the width of the lens, most of the surrounding events of a video recording or photograph are lost or outside the lens angle.

The physical position of the person taking the pictures or video recording can also skew perceptions. Most photographers know that they can position themselves in such a way that the photo tells a different story than what's actually being photographed. For example, you may have seen those pictures of a sunset and the open back hatch of an automobile. The position of the photographer can make it look like the waning sun is moving into the back of a vehicle, or, because of the spot where a picture is taken, it can look like someone is holding the moon in both their hands or lifting a star with one hand.

To have the awareness needed to cause such a display is a beautiful art. And yet, by accident, by coincidence, by craftiness, the same can happen with photojournalism and live broadcasts. To illustrate how this can easily be done,

Francis Schaeffer, a Christian apologist, put together a series of classes that were filmed-for-effect in 1977. The series was called *How Should We Then Live?* and addresses philosophy, art, media, worldviews, and much more. The cinematic version is based on his book of the same name.

In one of the segments, Schaeffer presents a single staged riot that is filmed and broadcast from two angles, with two different news commentators reporting the incident (Schaeffer [1977] 2017).[14] Media angle has much to do with how one perceives who is in the right and who is in the wrong. One visual perspective shows the rioters appearing to be abused by the police and the commenter affirming that notion. The other position makes it look like the law enforcement officers are being violently and ruthlessly assaulted by the rioters, and the second announcer upholds that assessment. It's a very instructive presentation that reminds us to always ask ourselves, and others, "Are there other reasonable explanations to what we are seeing on this or that clip? Is there more to the

14. It's easy to find the video of this scene online. It's worth taking the time to watch it more than once, noting as many details as possible from both angles. It's also important to pay attention to the littlest details.

story? Are there more details just outside of the range of the camera? Is it possible that this video angle may be giving us a slanted perspective?" It encourages us to think through ways to verify if a presentation is being reasonably objective or is it less so.

The visual angle of a recording device captures a limited optical area. The area outside of the lens's viewpoint is excluded and only what is within range can be recorded. Two cameras running at different positions recording the same event might give one a better perspective of what happened. Due to the partial range of the video, the direction of the recording can only give a limited perspective, such as when an on-scene reporter in a hurricane is the center of the video. You get the sense of the raging storm, but you aren't allowed to be distracted by everything that's flying about, flapping, waving, or ripping apart, until the street sign comes blowing into the video range, mowing down the reporter, to everyone's utter surprise, and even to the shock of the cameraman. Media angle is an important aspect to take into account when assessing a news event.

Additionally, there is a newer feature to mull over when assessing visual angle. If you like *America's Got Talent* (AGT), then you may recall this set of performances. There was a graphic video team using AI that waltzed onto stage with a handsome performer who had been on AGT previously. A big video camera, like the kind you'd see in a television production studio, was pulled out. The focus is on the singer and the video is broadcast up on a big screen behind him. To everyone's surprise, the video has produced Simon Cowell. The visual overlay is so precise that as the singer is singing it presents "Simon Cowell" singing on the screen. It's nearly flawless. It makes great entertainment, especially if you like having fun at Simon's Cowell's expense.

It is also alarming. If this can happen in entertainment, it can happen in other ways, some meant to mislead and other ways that are even more sinister. It's called *deepfakes,* where the producers of a video use AI and deep learning to create fake events that appear legitimate. It can be done to audio recordings as well. The *Guardian* has a quick article on the issue, "What are deepfakes—and how can you spot them?"

(Sample 2020). In that article, the author chronicles some of the most egregious examples of the way deepfake videos have shifted stock prices, influenced voters, and incited religious tensions. The *Guardian* journalist warns that this could accelerate a zero trust society that no longer cares to research and distinguish truth from falsehood. Real reality can become the victim of plausible deniability.

The point of this chapter should be clear: Visual angle affects what you see. Inattentive blindness is part of that visual angle, whether your own or the journalist's. There are forces afoot that may take the angle in darker directions. The right approach for receivers of the news is to recall that accusation, even graphic accusation, does not equal guilt. Therefore, assuming innocence until proven guilty, and remembering the possible incompetence (over malice) of the one reporting. Therefore, it is better to suspend judgment until you gain collaborating confirmations. Also, ask questions. Are there other reasonable explanations? Is there more to the story than recorded? Does the position of this photo or that video change the story in any way? Therefore, it's always important to validate before you palpitate, and authenticate before you propagate. We don't want real reality to become a casualty of deniable plausibility!

One other concern is regarding overreporting, to which we now come.

Practice for the Week:

- Find a social media video alleging to be a firsthand report of an incident. Check the video's details against other sources to get as many of the specifics as straight as possible. Write out a list of what is in the video, what is missing, from which side of the incident the video is recording, and any narrator comments that "interpret" the scene. Watch for inattentional blindness in the reporter, and in yourself. Write all this down in your journal.
- Take a random newscast. Follow the same approach as above.
- If you have access to the Internet, do a search on deepfake videos. Only watch one or two. Ask yourself how this has created a counterfeit out of a genuine

recording. Discuss with someone what you found.

- Practice suspending judgment on any of your news intake this week. Take them as details and possibilities but defer any actions or decisions. If one of the incidents grabs your heart, look for other reasonable explanations and search out more facts about the account. After three or four days, decide, based on what you now know, what you should do, if anything.

OVERREPORTING

Accusation Does Not Mean Guilt
Guilty until Proven Innocent?
Suspend Judgment
Hanlon's Razor
Human Reporters
Reasonable Explanations
Media Angle
Over-Reporting

I have two stories from when I was running an elementary correctional facility at Homestead Air Force Base in southern Florida in the late 1980s. To begin, my normal residents were men and women who were on their last leg in the military, usually due to alcohol abuse or out-right noncompliance to Air Force standards or the Uniform Code of Military Justice (UCMJ). Occasionally, I would end up housing people who had other problems, and their leaders had no idea what to do with them and simply charged them with deviancy. One such case was Airman First Class (A1C) Wiggle.[15]

Most of the details behind why she was sent to me have faded from memory. But what I do recall is that she wasn't involved with alcohol or moral failure. She had problems showing up for duty in a timely manner and sometimes wouldn't show up at all. After A1C Wiggle had been in my facility for two weeks, she began to voice suicidal desires. I got her in to see the base psychologists several times. But each appointment ended with her being returned to my facility with the attending psychologist asserting that the airman was not suicidal. Then things began to get worse, and the situation intensified.

In one of my final interactions with A1C Wiggle, it was clear she had a plan to take her life and was beginning to settle on her action. I asked her where she picked up the ideas on what to do, and she started describing a show she had seen on TV, which gave her advice on the actions to take, and even how to send letters to her family. In the end, I was able to persuade the Vice Group Commander that she exhibited

15. Yes, I've changed the name to cover up the person's identity.

all the signs of suicide and would be taking steps that night. She was admitted to a suicide ward by his order. A year later, she returned to thank me for taking the steps to intervene and getting her the help she needed.

Because of my experiences with A1C Wiggle, I began reading up on suicide. At that time, it was a significant problem at the Homestead AFB, where several enlisted individuals and officers had taken their lives. I began reading works like *Suicide Clusters* by Loren Coleman, published in 1987. While reading that work, I was captured by the relationship between suicide clusters[16] and media attention. The correlation between media reports about suicides and the rising number of suicides was shocking.

Eventually, we had another life-ending incident on the base. My new supervisor, the Group Commander, had called me to his office for a debriefing on my correctional facility and its residents. It was during this conversation he began to express deep concerns about the number of people who had taken their lives or made

16. *Suicide clusters*, according to the Center for Disease Control, is a higher-than-expected number of cases where people take their own lives or make clear attempts to do so, in a geographic area or in a given space of time. https://www.cdc.gov/suicide/resources/suicide-clusters.html

attempts. I reported to him what I had been reading on the subject, the relationship between how these incidents were reported and the way it seemed to encourage suicide clusters. He was fascinated and began to grill me on all the details. I gave him all the information I had, and the meeting finally came to an end.

Then came the next suicide. This time, however, the Group Commander put stipulations on how it was reported, and the way people could show their respects and mourn. The news of the event was subdued, and the cycle of suicide clusters appeared to have been broken. There was not another incident the last year I was stationed at that base.

I recount these two very personal incidents to call attention to the role of overreporting. In the 1980s until the present, most media outlets have begun to take ownership of the importance of not reporting more details than is essential when it comes to a person ending their life. For example, instead of describing the method and location of the suicide, they simply state the person has taken their life and keep information about the location more general. Also, keeping personal details generalized, not sensationalizing the particulars in headlines, and placing the story deeper in the paper or newscast, are other ways they ensure they are not overreporting.[17]

Overreporting works like a viral contagion. Whatever is excessively reported becomes primary in people's minds, whether it's crimes or war or tragedies, and the effects spread. Overreporting also includes the actions of news consumers—you and me. Not only can the media make too much of an event, but we also become accomplices when we start sharing and spreading the stories in our social media venues or personal conversations. But most often, on our social media platforms. We must take responsibility for our part in spreading the details and overreporting events.

We know how this works regarding suicide clusters, but we often are blind to the way it affects other troubles, such as mass shootings and terrorism. In the remainder of this chapter, we will focus on those two problems, see how overreporting accelerates the numbers and actions, and then notice how our own

---

17. For more details, I recommend you go to: https://reportingonsuicide.org/ They have a printable flyer to use with several helpful suggestions.

contagion-spreading activities become part of the trouble.

Mass Shootings

With mass shootings, there is intent by the shooter, as noted by their detailed plans of action. The person also has the capability in that they have access to weapons and ammunition or other weapons. The individual has opportunity since the assault is rarely a "flash" event. They look for places where people are gathered so that they can achieve the greatest number of deaths in a specific geographic location in the shortest amount of time. Oddly enough, a majority of shooters have no exit plan. This means that mass shootings, most often, are murder-suicides. There's very little we can do about those three areas—intent, capability, and opportunity—especially as a society and country built as a democratic republic, such as ours.

There is, however, at least one area we have some control over that has a significant influence on these murder-suicides, and that is over-reporting. In 2017, the National Institutes of Health wrote an article titled "Mass Shootings: The Role of the Media in Promoting Generalized

Imitation" (Meindl and Ivy 2017). In that article, authors James Meindl and Jonathan Ivy note that,

> "When mass shooters imitate other mass shooters, they are generally not imitating personally observed events (although this is possible in gang-related instances). In each case in which the event is unobserved, all information that could serve as a model for imitative behavior was provided via various media sources (legacy media, social media, new media), and research has demonstrated that media can influence imitation. Not only do people often imitate behaviors that are portrayed in the media, the "reality" of the portrayal does not seem to have a significant influence. Imitation can occur regardless of whether the model is presented live, whether it is presented via film, or even

> when the model's behavior is
> merely described."

The mass shooting pattern follows the pattern of suicide clusters. Overreporting can be contagious. In fact, two professors in Minnesota, Jillian Peterson and James Densley, have compiled a long-range and comprehensive database of mass shooters, which they have pulled together and presented to the public as *The Violence Project*.[18] They have written a book by the same name. One of the major traits they have observed is that mass shooters are fame seekers and copycats, which means that when media and social media engage in massive reporting on these traumatic events, it throws accelerant on a shooter's actions.

What is meant by *accelerant*? When making epoxy or working with fiberglass, you have *resin*, which is a sticky substance that has adhesive qualities. To make the resin stiffen so it can consolidate and become firm, you have to add an *accelerant*, a hardener. The hardener takes what is already at work in the resin and quickens its properties to become solid and set. For those who have become susceptible or

18. https://www.theviolenceproject.org/

vulnerable to self-destructive tendencies, often due to mental health issues, family failures, and crises in their lives, overreporting becomes a hardener, an accelerant. There's more to that story. In the interlude following this chapter, I take the time to review Peterson and Densley's book *The Violence Project*, which will give readers more features on their work, and on this accelerant process.

The same pattern of overreporting becoming an accelerant for mass shooting has been noticed in an article published by the National Center for Health Research in 2019. In the article "Does Media Coverage Inspire Copy Cat Mass Shootings?" the authors remark, "Shooters still get enormous attention: their names, photos, motivations, and stories are often shared for days following the event. The American Psychological Association points out that this 'fame' is something that many mass shooters desire. This sometimes inspires a copycat shooting, where the potential shooter typically tries to kill more people than their predecessor" (Pew, et al. [2019] 2022).

More research on the relationship between overreporting and mass shootings was done by

Michael Jeter from the University of Australia and Jay Walker from Old Dominion University. They presented a discussion paper to the IZA Institute of Labor Economics in 2018 called "The Effect of Media Coverage on Mass Shootings." In this study, they trimmed their search down to one major news outlet, a legacy media news source. Jeter and Walker charted the number of mass shootings, but they also plotted out when a report on a shooting incident was broadcast and how many days elapsed before the next mass shooting happened. Then, to give themselves something to compare and ensure they're not reading into the connections, they watched to see if the numbers of mass shootings stayed the same, rose, or declined when the news became primarily focused on wildfires and natural catastrophes. It's a fascinating read.

Their findings raise concerns. First, they found that as news sources were focused on reporting about a mass shooting, the next incident would usually happen seven to ten days later. Second, they noticed that when the news stories were primarily aimed at natural catastrophes there was a pronounced decline of mass shootings. Their conclusion was that media overreporting can be in the driver's seat of mass shootings. "Our findings consistently suggest that media coverage systematically causes future mass shootings . . . suggests that 58% of all mass shootings between January 1, 2013 to June 23, 2016 are explainable by news coverage" (Jetter and Walker 2018).

Those are critical statements from multiple researchers, but I would take this to the next level. Overreporting is not just a news problem. We add to it by oversharing the news and chattering about it, incessantly broadcasting it on our own social media formats. We can become part of the media overreporting. In other words, the more we talk about these incidents, the more we spread the sensational, high-arousal news reports in our public presence, the more we are part of adding hardener, accelerant to future tragedies.

One way we can move beyond outrage in the area of mass murder–suicides is by (1) not allowing ourselves to be consumed by the media's overreporting, and (2) to not become infected and spread the contagion in our own social media frames of reference. If overreporting is an accelerant, we don't need to add our own dose of hardener.

The same concepts on overreporting and its impact on mass shootings holds in regard to terrorism.

Terrorism

When I first joined the Air Force, I was being trained for the Security Police. Though we did quite a bit of law enforcement preparations, including riot control and other aspects, a significant part of my training was in the area of security, detection, resource protection, and combat. It was during this portion of our training we were shown how terrorists love publicity and will often create deadly events that have little sense of correcting wrongs but are more focused on making a statement and getting publicity. The publicity not only gives them some sense of credibility, but it helps them to recruit. Terrorist and radical groups need the oxygen of publicity to thrive. If this is correct, then you can already begin to see how overreporting plays right into the hands of terrorist groups and radical movements and even aids their attracting new adherents.

The Royal United Services Institute (RUSI) is the United Kingdom's leading defense and security think tank. In 2020, Jessica White, a research fellow at RUSI, wrote a paper for that organization titled "Terrorism and the Mass Media" (White 2020). In that work she noted several aspects of how media overreporting aids terrorist groups and other violent factions. Some of the high points of her key findings are:

- "Mass media can provide the publicity which terrorists seek. There is widespread consensus that the media's reporting on terrorism does this, and there is a clear synergy between the media's desire for a sensational story and terrorists' desire for publicity."
- "Mass media can play a contributory role in amplifying negative impact. While levels of fear are difficult to measure empirically, this research found substantial theoretical agreement that the media can amplify the negative impacts of terrorism and collective levels of public fear. This is primarily due to its role in broadcasting the story to more people than

would have been immediately affected by the attack."

- "Mass media reporting can contribute to imitation of terrorism. Social contagion theory suggests that the reporting of terrorist events encourages the spread of terrorist behaviour among like-minded individuals."

These, and other significant conclusions, lead White to lay out crucial recommendations so that news can be reported freely but not in ways that publicize and aid terrorist agencies:

- "Journalists should be aware that discourse and the way in which media reports are framed can have an impact on levels of fear, the process of radicalisation and the threat of imitation. As with practices developed specific to other issues, such as suicide, responsible reporting guidelines should be defined for terrorism. Discourse and framing should be accurate, balanced, unsensational, and contextual . . . Journalists should be as objective as possible, examining their own preconceived biases and possibly unsubstantiated theories."
- "Reporting on terrorism needs to be proportionate. Overemphasising the threat

of terrorism amplifies its negative impact and may inadvertently advance terrorist objectives. Journalists should be careful of misinformation from terrorist propaganda, the government or other potential actors such as foreign governments. Misinformation is a serious risk to independent reporting and public understanding."

- "Self-imposed ethical codes of practice and responsible reporting guidelines are important to mitigate the negative impacts of reporting on terrorism . . . Responsibility for content is necessary, while remembering that editorial independence is essential to modern democracy."

Much of White's key findings and recommendations go along with my own training and experience in the military. The author's analysis also applies to parties that may not be terroristic but are extreme in their rhetoric and actions and seem to attract violence. The Unite the Right rally in Charlottsville, Virginia, in August 2017, was a good example. The rally included many groups who have agendas and aims that can lead to violence. Counterprotesters gathered and included other groups that foment aggravation and aggression as well. This two-day event ended in one of the rally attendants ramming his car into the crowd of counterprotesters, thus, killing Heather Heyer.

Whether one sympathizes with the reason for the rally or not, what I found intriguing and frustrating is what happened by the end of a week of twenty-four-hour reporting on the rally and deadly action. Every newscast, media source, radio broadcast, and social media post seemed to talk about this whole situation for days on end, or at least it felt like it because there was so much of it. Toward the end of the weeklong reporting and overreporting frenzy, I was shocked to read an article that explained the recruiting numbers for both the "right wing" groups and the counterprotesters had jumped, and the journalist was baffled by its inexplicableness. I thought, "You've given them so much free press and advertising for a week, why would you be surprised?!" I doubt there was any malicious intent in the overreporting, but there was definitely a truckload of incompetence.

As a matter of fact, even the Congressional Research Services, in two of its reports to Congress—one in 2018 and the other in 2020—has tied antifa's growing significance to the August 2017 event. According to their report, "Antifa groups in the United States have gained prominence following violent clashes between white supremacists and their opponents in Charlottesville, VA, on August 12, 2017" (Sacco and Bjelopera 2018).

More can be said, but the point is clear. Overreporting has a contagious effect, and when we add our own social media venues to the overreporting, we become a part of spreading toxicity. Whether journalists, janitors, schoolteachers, scholars, homemakers, and hotel clerks, we all have a part in helping to mitigate the spread of suicide clusters, mass shootings, terrorism, and violent extremism. We can be part of refusing to add any more accelerant, or we can continue business as usual and remain part of noxious transmissions.

It doesn't mean we don't mention these events, but that we take responsibility for the way we disseminate the stories, which articles, how often, etc. We make a conscious choice to not give applause or fame to those who do these things. Maybe we spend more time remembering the victims and the heroes, ensuring that only validated details pass through our fingers to others, and not overemphasizing these incidents. Overreporting can be contagious.

One last break, and then comes the wrap-up.

Practice for the Week:

- Look over the past month of news reports for articles on the same incident of mass shooting or a suicide or a terrorist action. Compare reports from five different sources, marking which are more sensational and prone to encourage overreporting and which are more sensible. Discuss your conclusions with your weekly group.
- Take a few minutes and rewrite one of the accounts as if you were the journalist. As you do this, take the time to put it as factually as you can without overstating the incident. Read your version to a friend and get feedback on (1) factuality, (2) verifiability, and (3) readability.

- Pick one item from your social media site that someone else has shared. Look for three other sources about the incident. Go back to the original account and evaluate its effectiveness in factual reporting versus embellished reporting. Ask yourself this question: Which of these versions could I share with my friends if I want them to have the better version of this event? Which of these accounts could I distribute to them if I wanted them to become alarmed or reactive?

FINAL INTERLUDE: THE VIOLENCE PROJECT

It's all the rage! Almost every news feed and social media venue broadcasts it, some with greater alarm than others, the glut of press it receives makes it feel like it's happening everywhere, every day, in every neighborhood. It's like a voracious beast that is growing and consuming all in its path. Pundits and professionals describe it as a simple, single-item issue that calls for a simple, single-item remedy and they have the cure-all-fix-all antidote. The trouble, however, is far more problematical, which means a healthy response will likely be at several levels simultaneously. Into this hazy fog of violence has stepped a new book, *The Violence Project: How to Stop a Mass Shooting Epidemic* by Jillian Peterson, Ph.D., Professor of Criminology and Criminal Justice at Hamline University, and James Densley, Ph.D., Professor of Criminal Justice at Metropolitan State University, both in St. Paul, Minnesota. This 240-page hardback is well researched, readable, reasonable, and worth the time.

I first ran across the book after the Uvalde school shooting in Uvalde, Texas. It was from an article at The Conversation[19] where I found the authors and was hooked as I waded through the sensible-minded way they looked at these violent events. Peterson and Densley have compiled as much data and facts as are available on mass shootings in the United States, going back to 1966. They employed the modern standard that defines *mass shooting* as an event that involved firearms and killed four or more people in a public place. At the time they wrote the book in September 2021 they found there had been 172 of these incidents in the United States. They amassed the details in a database and interviewed several survivors, living shooters, families of shooters, etc. Their findings are not only online[20] but printed out in this volume. What they did was not out of an infatuation with violence, but "to understand how we can intervene earlier to prevent mass shootings before they occur . . . to learn from the patterns . . . that can help us prevent more people from

19. https://theconversation.com
20. https://theviolenceproject.org

dying" (Peterson and Densley 2021, 14). They squarely hit their target.

The authors have found that there is no single problem, but four categorical areas that act like accelerants that influence mass shootings. They can't confirm that these four areas are causative, but they are clear that they show up too many times to be ignored. These four traits are: (1) many shooters have experienced childhood abuse and exposure to violence at an early age, frequently by parents; (2) nearly all have reached a critical, identifiable crisis point, and plenty of them are suicidal; (3) most of the shooters look for models they can identify with in their violence and are aided in their search by the unending media coverage of cable news, the Internet, and social media. Loads of these people are motivated by publicity and fame-seeking, but they're also helped through these venues to find someone to blame for their miserable circumstances; and, (4) when opportunity arises to carry out a mass shooting, they take it. The top two opportunities include easy access to firearms and to crowds of people in public places (16–17).

And, because there is no single problem, but four categorical areas that spur mass shootings, Peterson and Densley hunt down multilayered remedies. This is what I appreciated most out of this meaningful volume. Almost every chapter pours just as much ink into workable solutions as it does on what feeds the violence. And their proposed answers are not anecdotal or opinion-based, but all have just as much research behind them as does their analysis on the details that fuel the violence. For example, while chronicling the role of various media in giving potential shooters models and avenues for publicity, the authors describe ways media, and you and I, can starve the mass shooters of publicity. They spend a considerable time explaining how tools like "No Notoriety"[21] and "Don't Name Them"[22] are valuable approaches to take so as to siphon off the oxygen out of fame-seeking lungs, so to speak. The authors have truly made this a levelheaded work!

I was initially concerned that Peterson and Densley were going to promote strident gun control measures and antidotes. I was pleasantly surprised, when working through the

21. https://nonotoriety.com/
22. https://www.dontnamethem.org/

chapter on weapons of opportunity, that their proposals were not the normal, drastic ones mentioned in the pro-gun vs gun-control debates. The authors discussed "permit-to-purchase," RFIDs, "waiting periods," and a few other approaches. The way they addressed each was backed up by studies but also empty of rabid reactions. A reader may feel they don't go far enough, or that they're uncomfortable with the authors' recommendations, but the volume is not a "gun control" manual.

The Violence Project was just the book I was looking for! And to know that the authors have made many of their studies and conclusions available on their project website adds untold value to the volume. This is the book people need to read instead of listening to single-answer experts. I recommend this work to law enforcement agencies, legislators, teachers, pastors, podcasters, social media pundits, journalists, and whoever cares about the violence. This book is a must-read!

Now, back to the conclusion of our regular program.

MICHAEL W. PHILLIBER

IT'S A WRAP!

Once, when our boys were in the Scouts, we had the opportunity to watch a whole newscast at a local television station, in person. It's an experience that impacts the way you see media personalities for the remainder of your days. On one of the walls was a TV screen that showed what the watching world got to see, and our heads swiveled back and forth from the screen to the live news anchors. It was informative. Highly made-up, almost masklike, to keep their oily skins from glistening under bright, boiling lights, the presenters would go about their business reporting the news, while on the screen they looked relaxed and "normal." Then the weather forecaster waltzed up to his place and pointed to a green wall while looking at the teleprompter to know where he was pointing. On the television screen, however, he was pointing to a map that had been imposed onto the video broadcast version. On it went.

These were real humans, trying to make a buck, while talking to no one but a camera. At the end of the broadcast, when the news report signed off, the producer said, "It's a wrap!" Clearly, this was the sign that the broadcast was over and everyone could get back to being real and normal.

Similarly, we've come to the end of this book, and it's almost time to say, "It's a wrap!" But first, I want to remind any and all who have made it to the end of a few important items. The goal of this work has been nonpartisan. This is not about civil politics. It's not about conspiracy theories. It's not about skepticism. Instead, it has been about how we, all of us, can move beyond outrage. We can vet—analyze and process—media of all kinds in sensible, sober-minded ways that will help us to be stable and steady in a stormy and rambunctious world. Of all people, Jesus' design is for his people to be the steadiest people in our society.

Therefore:

- Accusation does not mean guilt.

- Don't assume one is guilty until proven innocent, but rather that they're innocent until proven guilty.
- Suspend judgment and get more details.
- Employ Hanlon's razor: Don't ascribe to malice that which is adequately explained by incompetence.
- Reporters are human, with all that this means including biases, inattentional blindness, limited experiences, etc.
- Look for other reasonable explanations.
- Always keep in mind the media angle, whether visual or verbal.
- Beware of overreporting. Don't add to the problem but be part of the remedy.

We don't want to be played by malign forces, or marketers, or misinformers. Therefore, validate before you palpitate and authenticate before you propagate.

Before we close, let me share an interview I did with my friend who worked for the FAA. I mentioned him back in chapter 6. His experiences of investigating aircraft accidents and putting out press releases to the media reminds us of some of the reasons for this book.

Me: Lee, thanks for taking the time to meet and answer my questions. Tell me, what did you do in the FAA?

Lee: Aviation accident and incident investigation involving Air Traffic Control (ATC).

Me: Could you explain what some of your work entailed?

Lee: Sure. Not all aviation accidents or incidents involve Air Traffic Control. If the flight is conducted outside controlled airspace there is no regulatory requirement for the pilot to contact ATC and, as it was so aptly put, "there is neither the authority nor the responsibility for Air Traffic Control to provide services." Operations at small airfields without ATC towers, cropdusting operations, and cross-country flights at lower altitudes under visual flight rules (VFR) are examples of non-ATC flight operations. But, if an aircraft is operating inside controlled airspace and/or utilizing Instrument Flight Rules (IFR), then the Federal Aviation Administration (FAA) assumes the primary role in separating this aircraft from others in the system. In addition, the pilot of the IFR aircraft is responsible for maintaining continual radio contact and complying with all ATC instructions unless declaring an emergency.

Me: That's interesting. So, what happens, then, when there's an aircraft mishap? What was your responsibility?

Lee: In both instances—VFR and IFR operations—the investigation of an accident/incident is a process defined by regulations of the FAA and the National Transportation Safety Board (NTSB). Both accidents and incidents are fully investigated.

Me: You're making a distinction between an incident and an accident. Can you explain those a bit more?

Lee: I'd be glad to. The basic difference between the two is defined in FAA Order 8020.11C: an *accident* is an occurrence that involves death, serious injury, and/or substantial damage. (i.e., aircraft hits mountain). But an *incident* is an occurrence other than the above (i.e., aircraft crosses active runway without ATC approval, narrowly missing landing aircraft).

Me: What were you required to do? Were there different sets of protocols for an accident from an incident?

Lee: In the event of an accident or incident the agencies involved follow a defined and logical process as outlined in the above FAA order. Often, there is frustration from the public because of the time involved in conducting an orderly investigation as opposed to feeding speculation based on obvious circumstances.

Me: I see. They would both be investigated the same way. Can you give some examples of how the public's frustration might show up?

Lee: In many cases it would become obvious in the way the media hurriedly reported the situation. "This just handed to me . . . small private plane crashes just short of runway at the Metropolis International Airport. In our exclusive interview with the pilot of a departing airliner, he reports having no knowledge of any aircraft operating that close to his. No comment from the FAA as of yet, but controller error based on previously reported fatigue issues are suspected." Whereas the reality might have been that the small aircraft had departed an uncontrolled airport 10 miles west of the towered airfield. The pilot was not in contact with ATC, attempting to "scud run"[23] around

---

23. A *scud run* is where a pilot, so they can continue to see where they're going, lowers their aircraft's altitude to avoid clouds or other meteorological conditions that require them to use flight instruments.

controlled airports in marginal weather. He was not licensed or qualified to operate an aircraft in clouds or areas of limited visibility. True enough, the aircraft impacted the ground near a controlled airport, but the pilot had no intention of landing. In this example, the media's need to feed the public with speculation had a greater priority than reporting factual information. Admittedly, factual information is not the "low hanging fruit" for those reporters going live in . . . three . . . two . . . one . . . .

Me: Could you walk us through an investigation, such as in the example you just mentioned?

Lee: Sure thing. A proper investigation adds order in the midst of chaos and that takes time. In the above accident example, imagine the following:

- What if the deceased pilot had been frantically calling ATC on the radio, sadly tuned to the wrong VHF frequency. Investigation team members will determine the radio frequencies set on the aircraft's radios at the time of the crash. Other team members will listen to tapes of tower–aircraft conversations at the time of the crash to see if weak signals were received, or possibly, the pilot was on the correct frequency, but it was going unmonitored in the tower.

- Possibly, a local radio navigation beacon was off the air for maintenance. The pilot had attempted to determine his location by use of the beacon's signal. Was the planned beacon outage properly reported? Had the pilot checked the reports?

- Aircraft maintenance logs would show a recently replaced propeller. Crash site investigation team members will analyze airframe and engine remains to determine if they were properly working at the time of impact. Was this a controlled flight into terrain or loss of control because of mechanical failure?

- The list goes on. Other areas investigators will look into would be if this was related to something medical (heart attack or seizure), was the pilot impaired (alcohol or drugs), or was there interference by another person in the aircraft?

Even though these examples are being conducted simultaneously, they generally take more time than the public is willing to allow. By the time pathology reports and mechanical tests are conducted this will be old news.

Me: That's a thorough investigation. It clearly requires a serious investment of time. I can see where haste of public interest and hurriedness of reporting would make the situation frustrating.

Lee: Yes. In fact, one of the most difficult aspects of participating in investigations is the unrelenting "water torture" drip of outside interests—the press—using situations and speculations to meet their own deadlines and priorities. In my years of experience, it seemed that if the findings didn't support the previous story on controller fatigue, then the press will just fill the space with another story. Anyway, we go live in three . . . two . . . one . . . .

Me: Lee, thank you so much for your time and insights. This was very helpful.

Based on my friend's experiences voiced in this interview, I think we can see several aspects that make this book essential. Since justice takes time, usually longer than emotions last—and since there's often more to the story, which will take time to surface—then, we need to become more stable and steadier. We need to move beyond the outrage that makes us an easy mark. To do our part to not allow passions to wrest the scepter of reason from our grasp. We must validate before we palpitate and authenticate before we propagate.

We come to the end of this book, but not to the end of our responsibility. Hopefully you have gained tools to use to aid you in analyzing what comes through all the various media. And hopefully, in the present atmosphere of anger and anxiety you can move beyond outrage. It's a wrap!

BIBLIOGRAPHY

Berger, Jonah, and Katherine L. Milkman. 2012. "What Makes Online Content Viral?" *Journal of Marketing Research* 49 (2): 192–205.

Bursch, Douglas S. 2021. *Posting Peace: Why Social Media Divides Us and What We Can Do About It*. Downers Grove: InterVarsity Press.

Charky-Chami, Nichole. 2019. *Medium*. August 27. Accessed November 23, 2022. https://medium.com/@nicolecharky/heres-some-thing-most-news-reporters-won-t-admit-in-public-the-devastating-mistakes-b6cf-cec72c94.

Cooney, Elizabeth. 2021. "Health." *STAT*. April 6. Accessed November 22, 2022. https://www.statnews.com/2021/04/06/1-in-3-covid19-patients-get-neuropsychiatric-diagnosis-within-six-months/.

Crenshaw, Dan. 2020. *Fortitude: American Resilience in the Era of Outrage*. New York: Twelve.

Davis, Luke H. 2020. *Tough Issues, True Hope: A Concise Journey through Christian Ethics.* Feam, United Kingdom: Christian Focus Publications, Ltd.

Dodson, Jonathan K. 2020. *Our Good Crisis: Overcoming Moral Chaos with the Beatitudes.* Downers Grove: Intervarsity Press.

Ellyatt, Holly. 2021. "Health and Science." *CNBC.* April 7. Accessed November 22, 2022. https://www.cnbc.com/2021/04/07/1-in-3-covid-survivors-suffer-neurological-or-mental-disorders-study.html.

Gibson, Richard Hughes, and James Edward Beitler III. 2020. *Charitable Writing: Cultivating Virtue through Our Words.* Downers Grove: InterVarsity Press.

Hamilton, Alexander, James Madison, and John Jay. 1961. *The Federalist Papers.* New York: New American Library.

Hasell, A., and Briand E. Brian E.Weeks. 2016. *Partisan Provocation: The Role of Partisan News Use and the Emotional Responses in Political Sharing in Social Media.* Human Communication Research ISSN 0360-3989, Alexandria: National Science Foundation.

Henry, Matthew. (1706) 2022. *Christianity. com.* Accessed November 23, 2022. https://www.christianity.com/bible/commentary/matthew-henry-complete/proverbs/18.

Hutchinson, Christopher A. 2018. *Rediscovering Humility: Why the Way up Is Down.* Greensboro: New Growth Press.

Jetter, Michael, and Jay K. Walker. 2018. "The Effect of Media Coverage on Mass Shootings." *IZA Institute of Labor Economics.* no. IZA DP No. 11900. October. Accessed November 25, 2022. https://docs.iza.org/dp11900.pdf.

MacDonald, Jeff. 2021. *The San Diego Union-Tribune.* June 4. Accessed January 12, 2023. https://www.sandiegouniontribune.com/news/watchdog/story/2021-06-04/former-sdg-e-worker-sues-utility-for-firing-him-after-white-supremacy-accusation-went-viral.

Maier, Scott R. 2005. *ReasearchGate.* September. Accessed November 23, 2022. https://www.researchgate.net/publication/241655705_Accuracy_Matters_A_Cross-Market_Assessment_of_Newspaper_Error_and_Credibility.

Megan, Hunter, and Andrea LaRochelle. 2019. *The High-Conflict Co-Parenting Survival Guide: Reclaim Your Life One Week at a Time.* Scottsdale: Unhooked Books, LLC.

Meindl, James N., and Jonathan W. Ivy. 2017. "Mass Shootings: The Role of the Media in Promoting Generalized Imitation." *American Journal of Public Health* 107 (3): 368–370. Accessed November 25, 2022. https://www.ncbi.nlm.nih.gov/pmc/articles/PMC5296697/.

Moore, Shayne, Sandra Morgan, and Kimberly McOwen Yim. 2022. *Ending Human Trafficking: A Handbook of Strategies for the Church Today.* Downers Grove: InterVarsity Press.

Murphy, Sean, and Adam Boesen. n.d. "CSI." Accessed November 22, 2022. https://www.courtroomsciences.com/blog/litigation-consulting-1/how-to-deal-with-social-media-mobs-24.

Noble, Alan. 2018. *Disruptive Witness: Speaking Truth in a Distracted Age.* Downers Grove: InterVarsity Press.

Parrish, Shane. 2017. *Hanlon's Razor: Relax, Not Everything Is Out to Get You.* April. Accessed

November 12, 2022. https://fs.blog/mental-model-hanlons-razor/.

Peterson, Jillian, and James Densley. 2021. *The Violence Project: How to Stop a Mass Shooting Epidemic*. New York: Abrams Press.

Peterson, Jordan B. 2018. *12 Rules for Life: An Antidote to Chaos*. Canada: Penguin Random House.

Pew, Alex, Lauren Goldbeck, Caroline Halsted, James Castro, and Diana Zuckerman. (2019) 2022. "Does Media Coverage Inspire Copy Cat Mass Shootings?" *National Center for Health Research*. Accessed November 25, 2022. https://www.center4research.org/copy-cats-kill/.

Sacco, Lisa N., and Jerome P. Bjelopera. 2018. *Antifa—Background*. Report, Washington D.C.: https://crsreports.congress.gov/.

Sample, Ian. 2020. "What Are Deepfakes—And How Can You Spot Themare deepfakes - and how can you spot them?" *The Guardian*. January 13. Accessed November 25, 2022. https://www.theguardian.com/technology/2020/jan/13/what-are-deepfakes-and-how-can-you-spot-them.

Sasse, Ben. 2018. *Them: Why We Hate Each Other—And How to Heal.* New York: St. Martin's Press.

Schaeffer, Francis. (1977) 2017. "Mass Media Manipulation." *How Should We Then Live.* August 17. https://www.youtube.com/watch?v=N8qMi_VIuX4.

Shaer, Matthew. 2014. "What Emotion Goes Viral the Fastest? On Twitter and Facebook, Which Spreads Quickest: Joy, Sadness or Disgust?" *Smithsonian Magazine,* April. Accessed February 4, 2023. https://www.smithsonianmag.com/science-nature/what-emotion-goes-viral-fast-est-180950182/

Simons, Daniel S. 2010. "The Monkey Business Illusion." April 28. https://www.youtube.com/watch?v=IGQmdoK_ZfY.

Swasy, Alecia. n.d. "Setting or Chasing the Agenda: Who Controls the News?" *Donald W. Reynolds Journalism Institue Report.* https://www.ap.org/events/smw/down-loads/Report_setting_or_chasing_the_agenda.pdf.

Tosi, Justin, and Brandon Warmke. 2020. *Grandstanding: The Use and Abuse of Moral Talk*. New York: Oxford University Press.

Welch, Edward T. 2017. *A Small Book about a Big Problem: Meditations on Anger, Patience, and Peace*. Greensboro: New Growth Press.

White, Jessica. 2020. "Terrorism and the Mass Media." Occassional Paper, London: Royal United Service Institute of Defence and Security Studies.

Wollebæk, Dag, Rune Karlsen, Kari Steen-Johnsen, and Bernard Enjolras. 2019. "Anger, Fear, and Echo Chambers: The Emotional Basis for Online Behavior." *Social Media + Society* 5 (2).

MICHAEL W. PHILLIBER

INDEX

A

Acts

14:8, 74

22:4, 33

9:1, 33

Anger, ii, vii, 21, 25–29, 32–33, 35–38,

44, 67, 196, 203

Anxiety, vii, 23, 25–29, 32, 37–38, 67,

196

Awe, vii, 23, 28–29, 38, 75

B

Biases, 14, 109–110, 114, 174, 189

C

Caveat Emptor, 134–135

Christian Media, 116–117

Colossians 1:21, 19

Corinthians

1 Corinthians 10:31, 88

D

Deepfakes, 157, 201

Deuteronomy 17:6, 56

19:15, 33, 46, 56

19:16, 46

E

Ecclesiastes

7:21, 80, 103

7:9, 21

Exodus 23:1, 131

F

FAA, 114, 189–192

G

Galatians

5:19, 33, 46

5:22, 37

Genesis 3, 43

Grandstanding, vii, 30, 118, 121–127, 203

H

Haste, 115–116, 195

Humility,vii, 2–3, 35, 60, 63–67, 142–144,199

I

Inattentional Blindness, 151–153, 159, 189

Inexperience, 107, 114–115

Isaiah 33:5, 18

J

James

1:5,19

4:1, 77

John 14:6, 21

Justice, 18, 64, 72, 76, 91, 121, 131–132, 135–137, 161, 181, 195

L

Legacy Media, 167, 170

Luke 6:36, 59, 103

M

Mass Shooting, 168–170, 178, 181–183, 201

Matthew 18:15, 91

Media Angle, vii, 41, 51, 69, 93, 107, 129, 135, 145, 147, 150, 153, 155–156, 161, 189

Mob,48, 70, 72–73, 75–76, 80, 84

N

No Notoriety, 184

O

Outrage, i–iii, v–vii, 3–5, 7, 9, 11, 13, 15, 19, 21–23, 25, 27, 29–33, 35–37, 39, 41, 43, 47, 49, 51, 53, 55, 57, 59, 61, 65, 67, 69, 71, 73, 75–79, 81–85, 89, 91, 93–95, 97, 99–100, 103, 105, 107, 109, 111, 113, 117–119, 121, 125, 127, 129–131, 133, 137, 139, 143–145, 147, 149, 151, 153, 157, 159, 161, 163, 165, 167, 169, 171, 173, 177, 179, 183, 185, 187–189, 193, 195–197, 199, 201, 203

P

Peacemaking, vii, 84, 87, 90

Personal Perception, 150, 153

Peter

    2 Peter, 20

        1:1, 20

        3:17, 20

Proverbs

    11:27, 103

    14:29, 35

    15:18, 35

    16:32,35

    18:13, 47, 56–57

    18:15, 47, 56, 91

    18:17, 47, 56–57, 132, 139

    18:21, 47

    27:17, 3

R

Revelation 19:15, 33

S

Social Media, ii, 4, 7, 11, 13, 23, 25–26, 29–30, 32, 36, 42–43, 60, 73, 75, 79–80, 84, 87–92, 110–111, 116, 122, 124, 126–127, 130–131, 138, 145, 148, 159, 165, 167–168, 171, 176–177, 179, 181, 183, 185, 197–198, 203

Steel Man, 144

Suicide Clusters, 163–165, 168, 177

T

Terrorism, 165, 172–175, 177, 203

The Violence Project, vii, 168–169, 181, 185, 201

Timothy

1 Timothy 5:19, 46

W

Windshield, 123–124

CPSIA information can be obtained
at www.ICGtesting.com
Printed in the USA
JSHW022058190523
41904JS00002B/6

9 781633 572706